CULTURALLY SPECIFIC TREATMENT

A MODEL FOR THE TREATMENT OF AFRICAN-AMERICAN CLIENTS

Hattie Wash. Psy.D.

ISBN: 978-1-4834-8350-4 (sc)
ISBN: 978-1-4834-8351-1 (hc)
ISBN: 978-1-4834-8352-8 (e)

Library of Congress Control Number: 2018903957

Lulu Publishing Services rev. date: 04/26/2018

CONTENTS

ACKNOWLEDGMENTS

Special thanks is given to the following people for their support and encouragement as I struggled with updating and publishing the second edition of the Culturally Specific Treatment model: My daughter Nzinga Akila Wash-Knight, my grandson DeShawn Wiley, and my son-in law Boggest Knight. My sisters Dora Collins and Geraldine Taylor. Each of them in his or her own way was a driving force that enabled me to remain focused and committed. Michael Orleans, my African son, and my family in Ghana, West Africa. I would also like to thank the staff and consultants of EMAGES for not only encouraging me to publish but also for using the culturally specific treatment model as the foundation for servicing clients enrolled in the mental health, sex offender, and substance use disorders treatment programs. A special thanks is also given to Dr. Eleanor Harris for expanding the culturally specific treatment model to group services and for incorporating the group model into EMAGES's substance abuse and sex offender treatment programs. A special thanks is also given to Cherida Reynolds for developing the graphics for the cover of the book.

Dr. Edward Butler, a good friend who has been a supporter from the beginning of this journey. To Sheila Chew also, for her encouragement, as well as suggestions on ways to publish the book. Thanks is also given to Barbara Guion (my Philadelphia sister) for her encouragement and for making available quite time in her home, as well as to all the members of EMAGES board of directors for providing me a platform at the annual board of directors' retreat, where I was able to develop new ideas and approaches, as well as receive constructive feedback regarding the treatment of African American clients. A special thanks is given to Revenue Theodore Binion for her friendship and support over the years.

INTRODUCTION

Culturally Specific Treatment: A Model for the Treatment of African American Alcoholics was first published in 1988. My primary goal at that time was to develop a culturally specific treatment model that could be used by substance abuse counselors to treat African American alcoholics. The initial focus of the model was on the treatment of African American alcoholics; however, since its publication, the model has also been used to treat African American clients diagnosed with mental illness, sexual offending disorders, anger disorders, and situational adjustment disorders. In this publication, I am not only addressing the above disorders but also the treatment needs of African American clients addicted to illicit and prescription drugs, as well as the dually diagnosed client population, i.e., persons with a substance use disorder and a co-occurring mental health disorder. The primary client population, alcoholics, however, has not changed. The primary client population did not change because problems and environmental forces that contributed to a rise in alcoholism and drug abuse among African Americans are more prevalent today than they were in the 1980s.

Alcoholism and drug addiction among African Americans continue to be the number one health and social problem impacting many low-income African Americans. The crumbling of urban African American communities is one of the reasons that have been cited for an increase in addictive behaviors. The flooding of illicit drugs into these communities has also contributed to an increase in the number of alcoholics and drug addicts. The flooding of illegal drugs into African American urban communities can be traced back to the late 1960s and early 1970s. It was during this time period that suppliers of drugs began to bombard urban areas. Consequently, the large amount of targeted drugs that entered daily into these areas can be linked to the number of African American residents who become victims of an emerging drug epidemic.

The drug epidemic and the targeting of African American communities did not just happen by chance. In an effort to control African Americans during a time when they were fighting for civil rights and equal access to opportunities, as well as the upward mobility of many middle- and upper-class African Americans into the mainstream of America, drugs were used to keep African Americans as a group in a subservient position. It is this writer's belief that the United States government initiated a systematic attack to keep African Americans in their place by destroying various African American protest organizations and groups, such as the Black Panther Party. Additionally urban communities were systemically flooded\ with illegal drugs. This process was also an opportunity for drug traders to profit from an illegal drug market.

As indicated earlier, the beginning of the drug epidemic in urban African American communities can be traced back to the late 1960s and the early 1970s. It was also during this time period that the war on drugs policy of the United States was implemented. In 1970, President Nixon created the Drug Administration Office (DEO). In 1971, the "war on drugs" campaign was implemented and illicit drugs were classified as "public enemy number one" by President Nixon. The war on drugs policy had three primary goals: (1) to enter into partnerships and collaborations with other countries in an effort to control the supply and distribution of drugs into the United States; (2) to define and develop intervention strategies and techniques aimed at crashing the illegal drug trade and the consumption of illicit and illegal drugs by Americans; and (3) to implement policies, laws, and penalties designed to discourage the production, distribution, and consumption of illicit drugs. By the late 1980s, it appeared as if the war on drugs had only been successful in meeting one of the above goals: reducing the sale to and consumption of illicit drugs by drug addicts.

The arrests for drug offenses in the United States rose 126 percent, compared to 28 percent for other crimes. Also during this period, as well as today, the street dealers and their consumers, who are mostly

African Americans residing in urban settings, are the largest populations arrested and sentenced to long prison terms for drug-related charges. This is problematic given the fact that the typical cocaine user is white, male, a high school graduate, employed full-time, and living in a small metropolitan suburban area. The National Household Survey on Drug Abuse has revealed that 8.7 million whites used drugs in one month, versus 1.6 million blacks, and that white high school seniors are more likely to use drugs than black high school seniors. Additionally, 93 percent of white male users surveyed were more likely to sell drugs than black male users, 67 percent. White users also started using drugs at a much younger age than black users and continued to use them longer. Even though there is a higher percentage of drug use among white Americans, they are not being swept out of suburbia and into prison the way blacks are being swept out of their neighborhoods. According to Alexandra (2010), "One in three young African American men is currently under the control of the criminal justice system-in prison, in jail, or probation, or on parole—yet mass incarceration tends to be categorized as a criminal justice issue as opposed to a racial justice or civil rights issue (or crisis)." Alexandra (2010) further states,

> Drug offenses alone account for two thirds of the rise in the federal inmate population and more than half of the rise in state prisoners between 1985 and 2000. Approximately a half million people are in prison or jail for a drug offense today, compared to an estimated 41,100 in 1980—an increase of 1,100 percent. Drug arrests have tripled since 1980. As a result, more than 31 million people have been arrested for drug offenses since the drug war began. Nothing has contributed more to the systematic mass incarceration of people of color in the United States than the war on drugs.

Many Americans contend that the war on drugs has been unsuccessful except for the mass incarceration of African American males between the ages of seventeen and forty-five. There has been little to no enforcement by the United States government aimed at controlling the production, trafficking, and distribution of drugs onto the streets of America since the war on drugs policy was implemented; this is especially true for the drug cocaine and its derivative crack cocaine, which are the drugs of choice for many African American addicts.

A common allegation that has been made regarding the production and distribution of crack cocaine is that beginning in the 1980s, urban areas become the market and dumping ground for this drug. It is also alleged that the dumping of crack cocaine into urban areas was a primary contributor to the current drug epidemic in those cities. Another allegation that has not been totally disproven is that the drug dumping was initiated and financed by the United States Central Intelligence Agency (CIA). In August 1996, the *San Jose Mercury News* published an article linking the CIA's contra army to the crack cocaine epidemic in Los Angeles. A number of articles followed in the *New York Times,* the *Los Angeles Times,* and the *Washington Post* that not only implicated the CIA in dumping drugs into urban areas but also cited their involvement with drug trafficking and distribution in France, Southwest Asia, Panama, and Central America, just to name a few locations.

The United States government denies that the CIA had an official role in drug trafficking and marketing. However, there are those who do admit that in order for the United States to oppose communism, spread democracy, attract new allies, and reduce social revolutions in the world, the CIA has had to provide financial support to countries known to be involved in drug production and trafficking into the United States. Other forms of support that have been given to these countries by the CIA include plans, pilots, and protection. They have also aided some governments with the overthrowing of dictators who oppose policies of the United States.

The increased availability of crack cocaine in cities during the late 1970s and 1980s highlighted the substance abuse treatment field's inability to service this new emerging client population of crack cocaine and poly-drug abusers and addicts. Historically, the substance abuse field had provided treatment services to two client populations: alcoholics and heroin addicts.

Heroin addicts were treated primarily by state-funded outpatient methadone clinics with a belief that these addicts would be on methadone for the rest of their lives. Methadone clinic began emerging during the late 1960s and early 1970s. These clinics were also a part of Nixon's war on drugs. Methadone was the treatment of choice for heroin addicts; this was primarily due to the fact that the body metabolizes methadone differently than it does heroin. When methadone is taken regularly, it builds up and is stored in the body. Once a person is stabilized on methadone, a single dose can last from twenty-four to thirty-six hours. Addicts who are stabilized on methadone are not physically sick, and their cravings for heroin are reduced. It was this fact that led to the belief that crimes associated with drug addiction would decrease.

Clients prescribed methadone are expected to report to a methadone clinic daily and drink methadone while being observed by a dispensing nurse. Clients who are able to provide clean urine drops under clinic supervision are able to carry bottles of methadone home in lieu of reporting to a clinic daily. In addition to methadone maintenance, some clinics offered their clients individual and group counseling services, as well as assistance in finding employment and housing.

Alcohol treatment, on the other hand, dates back to the 1930s, when Bill W. and Dr. Bob founded Alcoholic Anonymous as a solution to alcoholism. Prior to the 1930s,, alcoholism was seen as a moral failing, and the medical profession believed it to be a condition that was both lethal and incurable. However, it was not until the late 1980s that the American Medical Association classified alcoholism as a disease. The classification of alcoholism as a disease was done primarily to assure reimbursement to insurance companies for treatment. There are many professionals who believe that alcoholism does not fit the definition of a disease, especially since it is self-inflicted. However, once alcoholism was classified as a disease, more treatment services for alcoholics were made available. Alcohol services were provided within mainstream outpatient and inpatient treatment programs, as well as in hospitals, social service agencies, and health centers. The majority of treatment facilities established during this period, however, required clients to attend Alcoholic Anonymous as an adjunct to their substance abuse treatment services.

Although alcoholism was classified as a disease, there was no agreement in the field during the 1970s relative to the cause, treatment, or prevention of alcoholism. The substance abuse field did not have its own philosophy or methodologies for the treatment of alcoholism outside of Alcoholics Anonymous. Historically, persons who were addicted to illicit drugs were classified as drug addicts and/or criminals, and persons addicted to alcohol were seen as sick and suffering from a disease. Because the early counselors employed by both the alcohol and drug treatment programs were recovering alcoholics and drug addicts, coupled with an operational belief that drug addicts were criminals and alcoholics were sick, tension between alcohol and drug counselors developed. A hierarchy soon emerged between the two, with drug counselors being at the bottom. It was not until the late 1980s that alcoholism and drug addiction were viewed as having a common denominator and classified as substance abuse disorders. However, the substance abuse field did not develop as a separate or distinct field with its own philosophy, treatment approaches, and techniques, such as a one-stop shop treatment approach, motivational interviewing, and culturally specific treatment approaches, until the late 1980s and early 1990s.

During this period, there emerged a general belief among treatment providers, many being recovering alcoholics and heroin addicts, that addiction was the same for everyone and therefore all clients should receive the same type of services: methadone for drug addicts and Alcoholics Anonymous for alcoholics. This belief and approach to treatment were problematic because the crack cocaine and poly-drug abusers and addicts who were entering the treatment system did not look like the heroin addicts or alcoholics of the past. Historically, the majority of heroin addicts and alcoholics had used drugs or drunk alcohol for most of their adult lives. Many of them had never entered the world of work or been integrated into the dominant society. However, this profile was generally not the case for the crack cocaine and poly-drug abuser or addict. Because of the rapid addictive nature of crack cocaine, many users became addicted after using the drug one or two times. Once addicted, the crack cocaine addicts, in most cases, lost their jobs, families, and savings within months of their addiction. Additionally, mental health problems that were once dormant begin to emerge among this client population. The substance abuse field was not equipped to serve this new client population or its underlying mental health needs.

Many of the crack cocaine and poly-drug users enrolling in substance abuse treatment facilities had underlying mental health issues that had never been addressed. This factor again highlighted the substance abuse field's inability to adequately service this new client population. Even though treatment for the crack cocaine and poly-drug user was challenging, clients who presented underlying mental health problems were more challenging.

The treatment needs of clients with both a psychiatric and a drug problem were different from the treatment needs of clients with only one disorder. Initially, these clients were classified as dually diagnosed clients. They were later classified as MISA clients, i.e., Mentally Ill and Substance Abusing clients, by the Illinois Alcohol and Other Drugs of Abuse Certification Board. Unfortunately, the MISA clients often fall between the cracks of the mental health and substance abuse treatment systems. Most counselors employed in the substance abuse field did not have training or experience in treating mental illness. Therapists and clinicians in the mental health field generally did not have the training or willingness to treat alcoholics or drug addicts. Most of the therapists and counselors in the mental health field had expertise in the identification, diagnosis, and treatment of psychiatric disorders but lacked knowledge and skills in the identification and treatment of substance-related disorders. As a result of the above, as well as voids in training and philosophy, clients who presented themselves at a substance abuse agency for treatment and disclosed a mental health history were systemically referred to a mental health facility. The same process described above occurred at a mental health facility whenever a potential client disclosed cocaine or poly-drug abuse or addiction. The frustration associated with attempting to engage in the treatment process for the MISA clients usually caused them to either avoid seeking treatment altogether or to only seek treatment for the disorder that was currently creating problems for them.

A main issue for both the substance abuse and mental health fields was the inability to determine which one came first—the mental illness or the substance abuse. Therefore, the general approach for admission to a mental health facility was based upon whether a person was currently experiencing psychiatric symptoms or taking a psychotropic medication. Admission to a substance abuse treatment facility was based on a person's addiction to or current use of alcohol and/or other drugs of addiction. However, if this same person began to exhibit psychiatric symptoms during the course of substance abuse treatment, the substance abuse issue would be addressed by the facility, but in most cases, the client would be referred to a mental health facility for mental health services.

Sequential treatment was the first and historically most common form of treatment for persons who were dually diagnosed. MISA clients, as indicated earlier, were treated by one system (mental health or substance abuse). It was believed by many clinicians that treatment for addiction must always be initiated first and that the individual must be in a stage of abstinence recovery from addiction before treatment for the psychiatric disorder could be linked. On the other hand, other clinicians believed that treatment for the psychiatric disorder should begin prior to the initiation of abstinence and addiction treatment. Other clinicians believed that symptom severity at the time of entry should dictate whether the individual was treated in a mental health center or in an addiction treatment center, or that the disorder that emerged first should be treated first. Because of the different beliefs held by professionals, MISA clients who were in need of both services received neither.

To address the dearth of services that were available for the MISA population, several substance abuse treatment agencies were funding during the 1990s by the Illinois Department of Human Services Division of Alcoholism and Substance Abuse (DASA) to address the service gap and needs of this underserved population. For the first time, integrated treatment was made available to the MISA client. Integrated treatment combined elements of both mental health and substance abuse disorder treatment into a unified and comprehensive program. Integrated treatment involves clinicians who are cross-trained in both mental health and addiction services. Case management and psychiatric services are also provided with integrated care. (Ries, 1995) However, most of the funded facilities that were providing integrated MISA services were defunded between 2009 and 2011 as a result of state budget cuts and have not returned.

A dearth of treatment services exists for MISA clients, coupled with a lack of training, experience, or willingness to provide services to the emerging client populations of poly-drug abusers and cocaine/crack addicts, as well as a treatment philosophy that views all addictions as the same. A philosophy that contends that everyone should be provided with the same type of treatment services. Complete abstinence was the goal of treatment for alcoholics and poly-drug addicts, and methadone was the treatment of choice for heroin addicts.

Alcoholics Anonymous was mandatory for alcoholics, and Narcotics Anonymous was the adjunct self-help support system that was recommended for heroin addicts. The clients' backgrounds, ethnicity, social and economic conditions, cultural differences, preferences, beliefs, attitudes, wishes, and wants were not considered important variables for treatment to be successful and therefore were not incorporated into the treatment process.

It was during the late 1980s that I and other African American treatment providers begin to realize that by not addressing the cultural history and background of clients, we were not treating the whole person but were instead treating the symptoms of addiction. Awareness of this fact forced many providers to acknowledge that the substance abuse field as a whole was not addressing the treatment needs of culturally diverse groups. This fact was particularly true for African Americans, who constituted a large percentage of the substance abuse treatment population. Many African American treatment professionals believed that the dynamics of black life and the societal forces that impinged upon African Americans' mental health daily could not be effectively addressed by applying traditional theories of mental health and substance abuse treatment to the African

American client population. It was believed that in order to effectively address the treatment needs of clients, treatment had to be provided within the cultural context of the client that was seeking services. It was within this framework that in 1988, I developed and published my culturally specific treatment model.

The culturally specific treatment model addresses the unique history of African American clients. It incorporates into the treatment process the culture and psycho-social development of African American people from slavery to present day. A strong emphasis is placed not only on the history of slavery and its impact on the current behaviors and patterns of African American people, but also on cultural carry-overs from Africa. This publication is an expansion of the Culturally Specific Treatment Model that was published in 1988.

The current publication is divided into four sections. The first section is a replication of the initial publication with updates and deletions. In the initial publication, the introduction section outlined the book's content, as well as defining the frame of references used in the development of the treatment model. The terms *European Americans* and *African Americans* were used instead of *white and black Americans*. The term *European Americans* applied to white Americans in general—i.e., the white middle class, Anglo-Saxons, and Anglo Americans. African Americans are defined as people of African descent residing in America. Members of this group are referred to as blacks, colored, negroes, Africans, Afro-Americans, and/ or Afri-Americans. The initial development of the model was normed on and designed as a treatment approach for lower-class, urban, African American alcoholics. However, because the treatment model's focus is on the history and culture of African Americans as well as the treatment of relationships, the model can be applied to most African American client populations. I found when updating the model that, ironically, all the information that was published initially is still applicable today. A primary reason for this may be due to the fact that during the latter part of the twentieth century, limited opportunities were available for treatment providers to receive training designed to teach them how to incorporate culturally specific treatment approaches, techniques, or models into the treatment process. A more serious issue was that there were a limited number of culturally specific treatment models and approaches that had been developed or published that focused on the treatment of African American clients.

Culturally specific treatment as a viable treatment modality had been embraced by the substance abuse and mental health fields during the late 1980s and early 1990s. Authors such as Sue, Sue, and Sue and Wash (1988) wrote articles and published books on the importance of culture in the treatment of minorities. It was believed that a more positive treatment outcome would result if focus was placed on cultural variables such as beliefs, values, identity, communication patterns, level of acculturation, language, religion, spirituality, and lifestyles. The above areas are addressed in section one.

Section two provides an update on the current thinking and status of culturally specific treatment models and the movement toward multiculturalism. Beginning in the 1990s, there was a consistent movement toward replacing the culturally specific treatment thrust with multiculturalism. An assumption of the multicultural thrust is that once counselors and others in the helping fields eliminate their knowledge gap and become culturally sensitive relative to worldviews, assessment, and acculturation constraints, treatment barriers such as language, beliefs, values, and family differences would be eliminated. Because of this belief, culturally specific treatment approaches and models that were developed to address the unique experiences of African Americans have been systematically replaced by either cultural diversity or multicultural models. The switch in focus is discussed in this section.

Section three incorporates an African-centered worldview into the treatment process for African American clients. An African-centered world view is discussed as a key component of treatment. The need for, the development of, and the incorporation of an African-centered treatment approach is outlined in section three.

Section four provides a culturally specific group treatment paradigm for African American clients. Included are also treatment planning, common problems in each relationship area, a case study, and a treatment plan for the case study.

SECTION I

THE CULTURALLY SPECIFIC TREATMENT MODEL

The culturally specific treatment model is designed for the treatment of African American alcoholics, as well as other African American client populations. The treatment mode empowers clients with skills that enable them to change and renegotiate their roles in four interrelated relationships. Counselors are required to be knowledgeable of the historical, cultural, and sociopsychological development of African Americans from slavery to the present day. The term *sociopsychological* is used instead of *psychosocial* because it is the author's belief that the social environment dictates a client's psychological development.

Treatment begins from this perspective and from an assumption that clients are able to define, interpret, and renegotiate their roles in each of the relationship areas via individual, group, and family counseling. During the treatment process, emphasis is placed upon presenting the problems at hand, as well as addressing negative behaviors and consequences that have emerged as a result of the problems. Clients are assessed and treated not just as individuals, but also as members of the African American community. Effective treatment is based upon the counselors' ability to define and interpret the relationship between problems presented by clients and the history and culture of African Americans, thus providing clients a frame of reference that is reflective of their lifestyles. All problems presented by clients are defined and interpreted within the cultural patterns, beliefs, and community-defined standards that African Americans have used to adapt to the conditions of slavery, racism, and discrimination.

One goal of the initial publication was to provide the field of substance abuse treatment with a model that could be used to treat African Americans who were suffering from alcohol abuse and alcohol addiction. As indicated earlier, the definition of the model defines its focus. The model is described as an instrument that is designed to provide clients with skills that will enable them to change or renegotiate their roles in four interrelated relationship areas. It also asserts that during the treatment process, emphasis will be placed not only upon clients presenting problems but also on negative behaviors and consequences that have emerged because of their alcohol abuse or addiction.

The frame of reference and definition for the model was developed after I attended Dr. Lewis King's presentation in 1984 at the National Black Alcoholism Council's annual conference. Dr. King stated that all life is continuous and can be understood and defined in terms of four interrelated relationships: physical/biological, traditional/spiritual, political/economic, and social/interpersonal. The above assumptions were used as the foundation for the development of the culturally specific treatment model.

Another assumption incorporated into the model is that client problems develop whenever one or more of the relationship areas becomes dysfunctional. Therefore, a primary goal of treatment is to empower clients with an ability to establish balance within these four domains. In order for this to happen, clients must first acquire self- and group understanding, as well as regain a belief in their own self-worth via African American history and culture. Counselors assist clients in accomplishing this task by defining and interpreting the relationship that exists between their present problems and African American history and culture.

African American counselors are required to have a working knowledge of the culturally specific treatment model, as well as an understanding of African American history and culture from slavery to present day. Starting with American slavery, however, does not negate African history prior to this period, nor does it negate retentions from Africa that are reflected in the lifestyles of African Americans. American slavery, however, provides counselors with a present-day context and a frame of reference from which the social and psychological lives of African American clients can be understood and assessed.

Examples of historical facts surrounding slavery that counselors need to know are as follows.

During the period of American slavery, African Americans used survival strategies and defense mechanisms in efforts to validate their identities and as responses to the brutality and cruelty of the slave system. According to Akbar (1984), even though African Americans are removed (at this point by five to six generations) from the actual experiences of slavery, the scars of this experience remain in both the social and mental lives of African American men and women. Akbar (1984), quoting Clark, argues that slavery, more than any other single event, shaped the mentality of the present-day African American. He further states that the attitudes and reactions that African Americans retained from slavery are extensive. Blauner (1972) contends that

> Slavery may be viewed as the third great source of African American culture … Here, under seriously restricting conditions, African Americans began developing their own communities and codes of conduct. Many persistent themes in the black experience emerged from the situation of servitude.

Additionally, both positive and negative adaptive modes of survival emerged during the period of American slavery. These adaptive modes of survival are reflected in the attitudes, behaviors, and lifestyles of African Americans. Karenga (1982) states,

> To know oneself is to grasp the essence of one's past, one's present, and especially one's future possibilities and thereby know who you are by what you have done and thus what you are capable of doing and becoming based upon past achievements and current conditions.

Today, as in the past, positive adaptive modes are used by African Americans to instill proactive, positive, and protective messages to their children and to each other. Throughout history, African American parents have provided their children with both positive and protective adaptive modes that are designed to be used daily as they interface with white America.

Positive messages are delivered mostly in the form of racial socialization. Racial socialization messages focus on the positive aspects and behaviors of the African American group. Instilling a positive self-image and commitment to the African American group is a primary goal. On the other hand, protective messages are designed to warn off the realities of slavery, racism, and discrimination. They also provide strategies on how to

5

effectively handle situations that can create physical and emotional harm and that may be life-threatening. The messages are designed to prepare children and young adults with information on how to stay safe and alive when confronted with racism and racial encounters from white America.

These protective and proactive survival mechanisms, as well as other positive adaptive modes developed during slavery, are incorporated into the treatment process. As indicated earlier, both positive and negative adaptive modes of survival were used by African Americans during the period of American slavery. Therefore, American slavery is not only viewed as a source of understanding and knowledge for counselors but also as a means of self-understanding and group identification for clients. The various modes of adaptation used by African Americans to adjust to slavery, racism, and discrimination are explored and defined by counselors during the treatment process. Problems presented by clients are viewed not as indications of individual deficiencies, but as ineffective adaptive modes of behavior.

The above protective and proactive adaptive modes of behavior are aspects of African American history that are not typically included in the treatment of African American clients. It is for this reason and other omissions of African American history and culture that the use of traditional theories developed by white psychologists to treat white people in most cases are not applicable to the treatment of African American clients. Traditional treatment models are based upon a Eurocentric world view. A Eurocentric world view tends to assess behaviors outside of the person. Identity and self-worth are viewed as external variables, such as how a client looks, behaves, and acts. The client is segmented into parts, and the material and spiritual worlds are separated. Additionally, traditional models were developed for the treatment of white, middle-class males from a dominant European American ethnic group. These male clients have good verbal and nonverbal communication skills and tend to be physically sound, healthy, and attractive. Their lifestyles, beliefs, values, and experiences tend to be similar to those of the therapist.

Therapists are trained to treat clients with the above characteristics. When these models and characteristics are applied to the treatment of African American clients, many incorrect assumptions about black life and behaviors are made. Deficient and inferior models emerge as explanations of those behaviors, and African American clients are shaped and pressured to either adapt to the dominant views on how to think and behave or terminate treatment. More than 50 percent of African American clients terminate treatment after the first session. One of the reasons for the large termination rate at the initiation of treatment is that most African American clients find that their culture, lifestyle, and behavior patterns are not incorporated into the treatment process.

TREATMENT ASSUMPTIONS

Three fundamental assumptions regarding the relationship between African American history and American racism are discussed in this section. The establishment of functional relationships for clients is contingent upon counselors understanding the history and system of American racism. It is important for counselors to be able to interpret the impact of racism not just on clients, but also on the larger African American community. A counselor's ability to integrate into the treatment process the relationships that exist between timeworn modes of adaptation to racism utilized by African Americans and clients presenting problems is essential.

The origins of American racism are discussed in assumption 1.

Assumption 1: African Americans are victims of racism, and racism affects all African Americans, regardless of their socioeconomic status.

American racism classifies one group of people as superior and another group as inferior based upon physical characteristics, such as skin color, hair texture, and the structure of the face and eyes. American racism also negates the uniqueness of the inferior group in terms of its history, culture, religion, art, philosophy, and worldview. It also violates the autonomy and self-determination of the inferior group and redefines the group based upon its definitions, beliefs, and standards.

American racism is firmly embedded in the fiber of American society and has provided the foundation for the classification of African Americans as innately inferior to people of European descent. It is this presumed inferiority of African Americans that has permitted people of European descent to treat African Americans as less than human. Racism underlies every facet of United States life, including politics, economics, religion, and society. Racism is primarily based upon a belief system of superiority versus inferiority that has been institutionalized in all aspects of American life; therefore, all African Americans, regardless of their social and economic status, are its victim,

European Americans have classified some African American civil rights movements as racist without having a clear understanding of the definition of racism. In order for a group to be racist, two variables need to be present: power and the ability to impose power. African Americans currently do not have the power or the ability to impose power on America's political, economic, or social institutions. Consequently, progress for African Americans can be classified as taking one step forward and two steps backward. In order to fully understand how African Americans historically were able to take one step forward and two steps backward, the historical development of institutional racism and its relationship to the African American group must be understood and addressed.

The context for American racism can be seen in European literature and religion. As early as the sixteenth century, racist attitudes and beliefs were projected in both the literature and the religion of the Englishmen, and it was these same attitudes and beliefs that were transplanted to America. Even before Europeans came into contact with Africans, they were writing about them in their literature. English scholars in their writings made distinctions between the colors of whites and black. The color white was described as reflecting, purity, virginity, virtue, and beauty. Black, on the other hand, was described as a reflection of evil, sinful, filthy, base, and ugly. Based upon the above definitions of *black* and *white,* Europeans defined and classified people of African and European descents. People who possessed white skin were viewed as superior and masters; black skin, on the other hand, was seen as inferior. The above descriptions were used by Shakespeare when he described the queen. "'Tis beauty blent, whose red and whites nature's own sweet and cunning hand laid on." His description, however, of his back mistress was the complete opposite: "My mistress' eyes are nothing like the sun; coral is far more red than her lips' red; if snow be white, why than her breast are dun; if hairs be wires, black wire grow on her head. I have seen roses damasked, red and white, but no such roses see I in her cheek." Gordan (1969), Wash (1988). The above descriptions of *white* and *black* are still found in most dictionaries and are the foundation for the accepted standard of beauty in America. American beauty is defined as a fair complexion of rose and white, which is the opposite of the color black. The above definitions are still projected throughout European and American literature and are used to determine one's status in America.

The Englishmen applied their definitions of white and black to Africans once they came into contact with them. Africans were perceived and classified as lustful and venomous. Shakespeare's play *Othello* is an example of how the Englishmen projected this assumption. In the play *Othello,* Shakespeare stressed sexual relations between whites and blacks by defining sexuality as blackness, the devil, and the judgment of God, who had originally created man not only angel-like but white.

The Englishmen's definitions of *black* and *white* were also justified by religion. Englishmen contended that the black skin color of Africans was God's curse on Ham (Cham) or upon his son Canaan and all their descendants. This curse was a sufficient account for the color of negroes. They casually accepted the assumption that Africans are descended from one of Ham's four sons, an assumption which became universal in Christendom despite the obscurity of its origins. The Englishmen also connoted the term *heathenism* to be anti-Christian. Therefore, heathenism in Africans was linked to barbarity and blackness. The heathenism in negroes was a counter-image of the Englishmen's religion as well as a summons to initiate an important distinction between the two groups. The fact that the Englishmen's culture gave birth to a negative conception of blackness independent of their knowledge of African people suggests that the genesis of white supremacy has its roots in the culture of the Europeans. The attitudes and beliefs established in England toward the terms *white* and *black,* and toward the white and black man, were transplanted to America and reinforced by its history and culture. American racism is an outgrowth of the foregoing process. The understanding of the attitudes and beliefs that were established and their impact on African Americans is imperative in order for treatment to be effective with African American clients.

Historically, racism within the United States has been practice on two levels: (1) individual or group and (2) institutional. The first form of racism consists of overt acts by an individual or a group of individuals for the primary purpose of causing death, injury, or destruction to property. These acts are usually televised and presented as not representing all members of the white race. The second form of racism is institutional racism; this form of racism is less overt, more subtle, and less identifiable in terms of specific individuals committing the act.

Unlike individual racism, institutional racism is embedded within systems that have been developed to perpetuate white culture with pervasive operations of anti-black attitudes and practices, which are reinforced and maintained by propagating the idea of a white superior group position. The institutionalization of racism within the United States can be clearly seen in the way that the slaves and their masters interacted. The relationship between African American slaves and the slave masters was defined based upon a system of superiority and inferiority. Doing this period, the most common form of contact between African Americans and whites took place on the slave plantations. African American slaves were classified, stereotyped, and molded in terms of position and expected behavior. This process was clearly demonstrated in the Alex Haley movie *Roots*. *Roots* showed the process of how African men were broken into slaves. Kunta Kinta was used to demonstrate this process. After a series of beatings and the partial amputation of a foot, Kunta Kinta was forced to abandon his African name, which connected him to a past and history, and accept the name that his slave master had chosen for him, which was Toby. During this period, the relationship that was established between the slave master and slaves became the model for race relations. The slave-master relationship was institutionalized and supported by the Constitution and laws of the United States. African American slaves were defined as subhuman, as a form of chattel, and assessed as three fifths of a man.

During slavery, a clear relationship existed between slaves and the use and abuse of alcohol on the slave plantation. The historical patterns of alcohol use and nonuse by African Americans have played a significant part in influencing African Americans' current attitudes toward drinking. African Americans were given mixed messages about drinking. Consequently, today they choose one of two extremes: (1) to drink heavily or (2) not to drink at all. Well-described patterns of drinking on weekends and on paydays are directly connected with drinking heavily in free times and drinking as a reward for hard work. On the other hand, religious slave masters prohibited their slaves from drinking because it was sinful. The above patterns of drinking were institutionalized on the slave plantations and evolve out of the slave experience.

The institutionalization of racism continued during the period following the Emancipation Proclamation in 1865. Prior to the Emancipation Proclamation, Abraham Lincoln in the famous Lincoln-Douglas debate defined the status of slaves as free men. He stated, "I am not, nor ever have been, in favor of bringing about in any way the social and political equality of the white and black race; I am not, nor ever have been, in favor of making voters or jurors of negroes, nor qualifying them to hold office … I will say in addition to this that there is a physical difference between the white and black races which I believe will ever forbid the two races living together on terms of social and political equality. And inasmuch as they cannot so live, while they do remain together, there must be the position of superior and inferior, and I as much as any other man am in favor of having the superior position assigned to the white race." The above statement made by Abraham Lincoln reinforced the status quo, and once again, race relations were defined in terms of superiority versus inferiority.

After African Americans were freed as slaves, a new phase of race relations developed between the white and black races. The stereotype of the happy, singing slave gave way to that of the "uppity," "insolent," "pushy" black who did not know his place and was out to compete with the white worker and rape white women. Even though African Americans were freed from chattel slavery, they were forced, by a failure of the United States government, to make provisions for incorporating the former slaves into the mainstream of society, into a new type of slavery called the sharecropping and indebtedness systems. Former slaves were forced back to plantations, where they were given portions of the land to work for their livelihood. Hence, former slave owners were able to institute an indebtedness system that became an economic substitute for slavery. Through perpetual indebtedness, African Americans were as securely tied to the land and to landowners as they were under slavery.

During this period, a whole set of new mechanisms aimed at repressing African Americans and instituting white domination were established. The first mechanism instituted was designed to restrict and limit the rights of African Americans. This was done by establishing a number of state laws aimed at nullifying the effects of the Fifteenth Amendment. For example, because African Americans were no longer deprived of the right to vote on grounds of race, a whole new system aimed at disenfranchisement was established, such as a battery of literacy and educational tests, poll taxes, and "grandfather clauses." In a few years, the overwhelming mass of African Americans in the South lost their franchise right, which was gained during the reconstruction period.

Racism was also institutionalized via the Jim Crow system. The Jim Crow system was designed to maintain white domination and to keep African Americans in their proper place. Jim Crow is the physical segregation of races based upon racial subordination. Within the United States, a multitude of laws and customs were established during this period that provided for the establishment of separate and unequal (or in some cases nonexistent) facilities for African Americans. Jim Crow laws were established in virtually every sphere of life. It became a punishable offense and against the law for whites and blacks to travel, eat, defecate, be buried, play, relax, and even speak together except in the stereotypical context of master and servant. This form of segregation was supported by the Supreme Court in 1896 when they passed the famous "separate but equal" decision in the Pleasy versus Ferguson case.

Racism in the form of white domination was also institutionalized. White domination was aimed at establishing fear and controlling the behavior of African Americans. White domination in the form of terrorism was used as a supplement to the other mechanisms of racial subordination that had already been established. Secret organizations, such as the Ku Klux Klan, were founded and resorted to intimidation, brutality, and murder as means of keeping blacks and whites who believed in equal rights for African Americans in their place. During this period, unorganized private citizens as well as the police played the role of vigilantes. The most notorious and extreme form of terrorism was lynching, but other tactics, such as beating, cross burning, masked night riders, verbal threats, hate rallies, public humiliation, and random discharge of shotguns in windows, were also used.

World War I and the migration to urban areas marked the first indication of new changes in race relations. African Americans migrated to the north in great numbers in response to the industrial North's demand for labor. As a result of the migration of African Americans to northern cities, more opportunities were open to them. World War I also exposed African American soldiers to conditions outside the South and overseas. At the conclusion of World War I, it was believed by a small group of African American intellectuals that both the impact of the war and the migration of African Americans to the North would positively alter race relations within the United States. The above belief was stated by W. E. B. Du Bois in an article in the crisis. He wrote that "out of the war will rise, too, an American negro with the right to vote and the right to work and the right to live without insult." The above expectations for African Americans, however did not occur due to a backlash of organized white violence, which was sanctioned by national institutions, both governmental and private. Additionally, returning African American veterans aroused hostility from whites, as shown by a wave of race riots and a rise in the number of African American men that were lynched.

At the end of World War II, African Americans' expectations were even greater for a deal, but as in World War I, they were met by white violence, which was often directed at the serviceman, who had been stirred up by the war. Unlike after World War I, there was an outcry against the violence, primarily out of political necessity. However, the real changes and opportunities for African Americans came in the 1960s as a result of mass militancy and the adoption of unconventional methods of protests, such as passive resistance and civil disobedience. As a result of this action, Jim Crow laws and other overt acts of discrimination were removed by law. Even though the obvious cases of gross discrimination and segregation was pretty much eliminated during this period, racism still remains. The political, economic, and social conditions that allowed racism to survive from one generation to the next are still present. Racism is less overt and less harsh than in previous periods, but it is real, and no black person can escape its grip.

As indicated earlier, racism, both direct and indirect, has been an integral part of American life for African Americans, and it is not a dying phenomenon. In various and subtle ways, racism and neo-racism permeate the political, economic, and social institutions of north, south, west, and east. Thus, the black culture movement is a reasonable response to the realities of a society that in its present socioeconomic and psychic state is not going to accept people of African descent without imposing a ceiling on their human possibilities.

The above fact is a primary reason why historically African Americans have taken one step forward and two steps backward. The United States has opened opportunities for African Americans, such as affirmative action and voting laws, as well as removing discriminatory laws in housing and employment. They have also propagated a belief that social class and economic status determine one's power and prestige in America and not race. However, African Americans are still fighting for their rights. This back-and-forth approach to progress has given the impression that racism is dead, which many Americans, both white and black, believe.

The belief that social class and economic status, and not race, determine one's power and prestige in American life has not proven true for African Americans. Thus, African Americans classified in the middle and upper social and economic groups are still victims of racial oppression, discrimination, and prejudice. This has even proven true for the first African American president of the United States. Because President Obama did not fit the image of a president for the United States—a "white" man—many white Americans publically stated that they would make sure that everything he proposed and passed would be rejected and appealed. Their goal was to discredit him as a leader of men. To this end, President Obama and his family have been publically disrespected, ridiculed, and put down. White Americans' opposition to him was not based upon his ability to lead the country, but on the fact that he was African American and not white.

It is difficult to convey fully to people who have not experienced racism the insidious, pervasive, and constant impact that it has on the lives of African Americans. In various and subtle ways, racism penetrates all social institutions. In the eyes of white Americans, race is the salient factor in relations with African Americans, and given the historical development of American racism and the fact that it is firmly embedded in America's culture, it is unlikely that racism will decline during our lifetime.

Consequently, African Americans collectively and individually struggle against it on a daily basis. African Americans' ability to survive and succeed in a society that has negatively stereotyped, oppressed, and excluded them from full participation in America reflects a legacy of resilience, self-determination, and cultural adaptation, as well as the strength of the African American people. An understanding, therefore, of the origins of American racism and its impact on African American clients is imperative when treating African American clients.

Assumption 2: Within the African American community, both individual and group adaptive and survival mechanisms have evolved in response to the conditions and pressures of racial oppression. The four most common modes of adaptation for African Americans have been the following:

1. To integrate or assimilate into the dominant society.
2. To reject the dominant society by embracing a black nationalist posture.
3. To become alienated from the dominant society.

4. To become marginal, i.e., able to move between the dominant society and the African American community.

Assumption 2 is based upon a belief that African Americans, in an attempt to overcome racial oppression and promote psychological and physical well-being, developed different adaptive modes of behavior and survival strategies both individually and collectively among themselves. African Americans also used the church, work, music, education, language, aggressive anger, alcohol, drugs, and crime to adapt to the conditions of racism and group oppression. African Americans' ability to quickly move between different adaptive modes of behavior and survival mechanisms reflects their understanding of a system which has classified them as inferior and treated them as second-class citizens. Their ability to effectively manipulate the American system by employing different adaptive modes of behavior is reflected in their economic, political, and social gains.

Historically, the two main political responses to racial oppression utilized by African Americans have been (1) seeking acceptance from white Americans via integration or (2) separation from white Americans via nationalism. Integration and nationalism as political adaptive modes of behavior utilized by African Americans can be traced back to shortly after the American Revolution. It was during this period that the conditions of African Americans were deteriorating, and many saw the complete withdrawal from America as the only way to obtain the rights, freedom, and opportunities they sought. Therefore, African American nationalists like Paul Cuffee and Martin R. Delaney, as well as prominent whites, advocated for emigration to Africa, the Caribbean, and Haiti. Some African Americans did emigrate during this period. Paul Cuffee transported thirty-eight (38) African Americans to Liberia in 1815. But the numbers of African Americans seriously interested in emigration or who were able to emigrate were small. Physical or political withdrawal from white Americans has been advocated by African Americans since the American Revolution (Sweets, 1976).

African Americans also utilized nationalism as an adaptive mode of behavior to withdraw physically or politically from the dominant society, as well as a method to change the social, economic, and political status of African Americans. African American nationalists in the broad sense are seeking either a physical or political withdrawal from the European American society. Golden (1971) states, "the concept of nationalism … may be thought of as the belief of a group that it possesses, or ought to possess a country; that it shares or ought to share, a common heritage of language, culture, and religion; and that its heritage … and … ethnic identity are distinct from those of other groups. Nationalists believe that they should, therefore, be in control of their social, economic, and political institutions."

Nationalism, as expressed by African Americans during the nineteenth century, can be best interpreted not as a pathological reaction to white racism, but as a sentiment that emerged from within the African American experience. African Americans were, according to Sweets (1976), "nationalistic about their color and about their capabilities, indispensable ingredients in self-pride and creativity … Blacks realized that they have a common history of suffering and oppression which differentiated them from other groups and that, as a prescribed minority, they had special interests and special needs which required them to band together as a unit."

African American nationalists have historically rejected the concept of integration. Their focus has been on the cultural and psychological oppression of African Americans with a goal of an economic, physical, or cultural separation from white America. African American nationalism can be divided into three areas: economic nationalism, cultural nationalism, and political nationalism.

According to Broom and Glenn (1965), the first important surge of African American economic nationalism came with the end of the Reconstruction period. African Americans' disfranchisement, coupled with increased segregation and the withdrawal of support by whites, forced them to seek racial advancement through self-help and racial solidarity. During this period, Booker T. Washington was the most influential advocate for self-help and racial solidarity. "Washington advocated the development of separate negro enterprises to lessen white prejudice and to help incorporate negroes into American society. However, he never publicly espoused social equality" Bloom and Glenn (1965).

A half-century later, Elijah Muhammad and the Black Muslims, as well as African American businessmen and economists, advocated for economic nationalism. They saw "capitalism, collective, or survival economic" as being the means by which the African American community could accumulate capital. Economic nationalism allows money to flow in a circle within African American communities.

The accumulation of capital is viewed by many African Americans as necessary if the needs of their communities are to be met.

The Black Muslims and African American economists see capital as being accumulated in a collective or a cooperative ownership fashion. This form of capitalism differs from the monopoly capitalism of western society because it allows money to flow within the African American community many times before it is passed into mainstream America. The Black Muslims practiced this form of economic nationalism. The money that the Black Muslim community accumulates through its businesses, publishing company, and other ventures is redirected into Muslim schools, mosques, and African American businesses. African American economists believe, however, that economic guidelines must be developed from a black theoretical framework that is based upon the experiences and needs of African American people and that the accumulation of capital is only the elementary stage in the struggle for black economic liberation (Wright, 1969).

Cultural nationalism is based upon a belief that African Americans make up a distinct cultural group with a common past, present, and, hopefully, future. Cultural nationalists believe that an understanding of African American culture would provide African Americans with identity, race pride, purpose, and direction. Cultural nationalists have, historically, challenged the myths and stereotypes surrounding African Americans. African American writers, for example (during the antebellum period), challenged the negativity associated with the generally believed notion that

African Americans were descended from Ham, one of the sons of Noah. Although they did not challenge the legend, they focused on discrediting the negative myth that African Americans inherited a curse from Ham by describing the accomplishments and successes of Ham's early descendants: "Among the descendants of Ham, they asserted, were Moses, David, Solomon, Socrates, Plato, Hannibal, Cesar, Pompey … Augustine, and Jesus Christ" (Bloom and Glenn, 1965).

Marcus Garvey and Elijah Muhammad (Nation of Islam) are known primarily because they advocated for the physical withdrawal of African America from European America. Both, however, were cultural nationalists. They operated on the belief that African Americans make up a distinct cultural group with a common past, present, and future. They, therefore, advocated for unity via race pride, self-help, and collective economics. They also advocated for the creation of social, economic, and historical institutions based upon a value system that is beneficial to African Americans.

Political nationalism incorporates the goals of both economic and cultural nationalism. In addition, proponents of political nationalism believe that African Americans must gain political control of their communities. Political nationalists believe that African Americans must compete and gain public office and that once elected to public office, African Americans can influence and shape government decision-making as well as advocate for the interest and concerns of African Americans. Various forms of political nationalism have emerged since the American Revolution. However, the themes of political nationalists have echoed the primary goal of nationalism, which is the economic, cultural, and political control of African American communities by African Americans.

Integration as a philosophy or ideology emerged after African Americans were emancipated from slavery. The advocates of integration sought equality for African Americans through the channels of democracy. Karenga (1982) states, "The integrationist thrust, in its political sense, was an effort to break down barriers to full participation in the US society and remove the penalty and other negative consequences of racial distinctions." The advocates of integration believe that African Americans can move into the dominant society if reforms are made in the economic, political, and social systems. This belief has been expressed through open protest and strategies aimed at gaining equal access to those systems that have excluded African Americans, i.e., the educational system via public and private education, the economic system via equal employment, and the political and judiciary system via public facilities and accommodations.

The organizations that have been most influential in propagating integrationist goals have been the National Association for the Advancement of Colored People (NAACP), the Urban League, and the Southern Christian Leadership Conference (SCLC). Each of these organizations has focused upon reforming an American system which has excluded African Americans from equal access.

The NAACP emerged from the Niagara Movement of W. E. B. Du Bois and other negro and white liberals during a period when African Americans were moving north. At its beginnings, the NAACP sensed that the status of African Americans in the North would not be significantly better than their status had been in the South.

The NAACP's primary interest was in political and legal power, with a major emphasis upon propaganda aimed at reaching the conscience of the American people (Clark, 1970). The NAACP, therefore, pioneered the use of direct action demonstration in an effort to improve the status of African Americans. Since its inception, the NAACP has fought segregation in public schools via the American legal system. The NAACP was responsible for a series of important legal cases that were brought before the Supreme Court, which eventually led to the 1954 Supreme Court decision *Brown v. the Topeka Board of Education*—the decision that desegregated public schools in the South.

The Southern Christian Leadership Conference, under the leadership of the late Dr. Marin Luther King Jr., was the first civil rights organization to start in the South. It began in Atlanta in 1957, primarily as an expression of the commitment of nearly one hundred men throughout the South to the idea of a southern movement to implement equality through nonviolent means (Clark, 1970). The Southern Christian Leadership Conference is best known for the series of nonviolent marches and sit-ins headed by Dr. Marin Luther King Jr., which desegregated public facilities and accommodations in the South between 1957 and the death of Martin Luther King Jr. in 1968. Dr. King and his followers appealed to the moral conscience of white Americans and African Americans. Dr. King effectively turned the main weakness of the African Americans (their numerical, economic, and political importance) into a working strategy—a strategy that sought justice for African Americans through the mechanism of nonviolence (Clark, 1970).

Integration and nationalism for African Americans are interrelated. The two approaches have been viewed as antagonistic based upon the strategies and approaches that each have used to accomplish their goals. Historically, however, African American integrationists have also been nationalists. They are integrationists in the sense that they believe African Americans can be assimilated into the political, economic, and social systems of the dominant society through the channels of democracy. They are nationalists, on the other hand, about their color and about their capabilities. However, due to racial exclusion, separate social and political conventions and organizations were established throughout African American communities. It was in these nationalistic groupings that allegations of inferiority received from white America were disproved and where addresses were given that acknowledged African American heroes and leaders—heroes and leaders that white Americans were denouncing or ignoring. It was also at these nationalist gatherings that African Americans could release their pent-up anger at a nation that refused to acknowledge their citizenship and contributions of blood, sweat, and tears to American history. Nationalism was practiced in the form of conventions, organizations, churches, sororities, and fraternities, which trained and demonstrated African American leadership, thereby instilling greater self-confidence and self-pride. It was these nationalist groupings that reinforced a powerful sense of community, commonality, common heritage, and group pride by enabling African Americans to establish traditions of value for themselves, which would in turn elicit respect from others (Sweets, 1976).

Since the abolishment of slavery, the integrationist and nationalist approaches have been modes of adaptation, as well as political responses aimed at eliminating the racial oppression of African Americans. It has been the failure of the above approaches to reach these goals, coupled with increased racial oppression, urbanization, and limited economic opportunities that has contributed to the evolution of additional adaptive modes of behavior and survival mechanisms. An additional adaptive mode utilized by African Americans in response to their social conditions and victimization is a perception of powerlessness and alienation from the dominant society.

During the period between 1910 and 1960, it was estimated that 4.6 million African Americans migrated to northern cities in an effort to escape the oppression of the South and their subordinate status. African Americans were especially attracted to the industrial centers of the North, where the demand for labor was great. Thousands moved to Pittsburgh, Cleveland, Detroit, New York, Cincinnati, Columbus, Philadelphia, and Chicago. By 1920, almost 40 percent of the North's African American population resided in these states. African Americans did not find relief, however, from oppression and discrimination in the North. They found, instead, poverty, disillusionment, misery, and segregation. As African Americans migrated north, European Americans intensified their actions to preserve American institutions and the supremacy of the European race. Racial conflicts and animosities increased as African Americans moved north. African Americans could not have anticipated the wholesale rejection they experienced in the North. Separate systems were established for African Americans in hosing, economics, politics, and education. Employment opportunities were limited and restricted to certain areas. European Americans, via the Ku Klux Klan, warned African Americans in the North that they must respect the rights of the white race, in whose county they were permitted to reside. Racial conflicts swept the country during this period, and neither the federal nor state governments seemed interested in effective interventions (Franklin, 1970).

It was during this period that a new system of victimization for African Americans emerged, i.e., ghettoization and indifference. In the 1980s, more than 55 percent of African Americans in urban settings lived in the cities' poorest neighborhoods. It was also during this period that some African Americans came to believe that their life chances were unequal to those of European Americans. Their poverty, coupled with blocked economic opportunities, created a sense of hopelessness and apathy. These African Americans have been classified as alienated.

Alienated African Americans are described as being preoccupied with maintaining life, sanity, and dignity in a society that has restricted their life chances. They have acquired lifestyles outside of the mainstream that allow them the opportunity to provide food, clothing, and shelter for themselves and their families. Alienated African Americans are also preoccupied with surviving both physically and emotionally in a society that has classified them as the "black underclass" or the "black poor." Pinkney (1984) states that "they constitute a significantly younger population than the poor of previous generations. These young blacks, some as young as thirteen or fourteen, are already earmarked for failure. They are often undereducated, jobless, without saleable skills or the social credentials to gain access to the mainstream of life. They are rendered obsolete before they even begin to pursue a meaningful role in society … most are eager for meaningful employment, but because of society factors, they have been abandoned to a life of hopelessness."

Poverty, lower-class status, ghetto living, and limited economic opportunities are problems associated with the alienated African American. Alienated African Americans perceive white America, the system, or "the man" as their problem. They believe that blocked economic opportunities and upward mobility are directly related to a racist system. Consequently, they have developed their own underground economy, which consists of selling "bootleg" merchandise, i.e., clothing, CDs, DVDs and drugs, just to name a few items.

Alienated African Americans have adapted to a lowered socioeconomic status and the problems that are reflective of their lifestyles. According to Pinkney (1984), members of the black underclass have carved out for themselves lifestyles geared toward minimizing the hopelessness and despair that are characteristics of their existence. Their associates are fellow members of the underclass, and their lives revolve around the streets, where they frequently become involved in illegal activities. Drug and alcohol abuse are widespread among the underclass. According to Pinkney, they serve to cushion a marginal and difficult existence.

Most of the adaptive modes utilized by the alienated African American have been classified as pathological or antisocial, i.e., crime, gangs, alcohol, and drugs. However, music, religion, and group and family solidarity are other common modes of adaptation that are also utilized by this group. Alienated African Americans do not view themselves as integrationists, nor as nationalists. Most of them support the goals of both groups. They are concerned with their human rights, economic and political justice, and group progress. Their daily existence, however, is focused upon survival. Historically, whichever leader or movement advocates their concerns receives their loyalty. The Marcus Garvey Movement of the 1920s, the Civil Rights Movement of the 1960s, and the Nation of Islam are movements that have included large followings from this group.

Another mode of adaptation for African Americans, which dates back to post-slavery, is the perception of being marginal. Unlike the alienated African American, whose life is defined by poverty, hopelessness, and despair, the marginal African American is usually a member of the middle class. The emergence of an African American middle class in the North developed as a result of racial discrimination and segregation in housing. African Americans were restricted from acquiring housing in European American neighborhoods; consequently, they were concentrated and contained in sections of northern metropolitan areas where services were either poor or nonexistent. African American services and institutions developed in response to limited opportunities and to meet the needs of the community. The church and schools became basic institutions in the community. African American entrepreneurs developed a variety of service enterprises, such as barber shops, beauty parlors, funeral homes, restaurants, pool parlors, taverns, and hotels. African American entrepreneurs sold to what came to be called "the negro market." Successful banking and insurance businesses also grew up within some African American communities. It was "the negro market" in urban communities that "provided an opportunity for the emergence of a black middle class of teachers, doctors, dentists, undertakers, realtors, insurance agents, ministers, newspaper editors,and small businessmen who attempted to meet the needs of a black community that whites were often unwilling to serve" (Landry, 1987).

The African American middle class has been classified as marginal or bicultural, i.e., able to shift back and forth between the two worlds. The lifestyles and aspirations of the African American middle class are similar to those of middle-class European Americans. The European American social system, however, has kept the middle-class African American "half in and half out." Pinkney (1984) states that members of the black middle class can possess the same degree of education, the same income, and the same occupational status as whites, but they are still considered black first and middle class second. Because they are African American, they will continue to live marginal lives in a deeply racist society. Most of them associate socially with other middle-class blacks, either because they have been rejected by whites, because they fear of rejection by whites, or by choice.

The African American middle class adapted to exclusion and deprivation by creating a world of its own. In this world, they are able to pursue their social activities and play their roles as race leaders with few feelings of inferiority or deprivation (Drake, 1965). The development of African American organizations, professional associations, and civil and social clubs are all concrete manifestations of the degree to which the African American middle class has been kept out of the social systems of mainstream American life. It further indicates that many African Americans have lost faith in the theory that they will be respected and accepted if they measure up to white upper- and middle-class standards. Some cite this as the central fallacy in the theory of racial integration.

Middle-class African Americans are more likely to experience racism than low-income African Americans. This is primarily because middle-class African Americans will encounter the white race more frequently than lower-income African Americans, whose environment in most cases shields them from white people. They are spared the discrimination of everyday racism that middle-class African Americans encounter in employment and public accommodations.

The African American middle class covers a wide income range, and whatever cohesion it has comes from the network of churches and social clubs to which many of its members devote a great deal of time and money. Their basic goals are living well and being respected as Americans. Middle-class African Americans are not concerned with integrating with European Americans. They want their rights and good jobs, as well as decent schools for their children (St. Clair Drake, 1965). Middle-class African Americans' goal is not to live next door to white Americans, but to enjoy the same benefits and life opportunities as their white counterparts.

Assumption 3

A primary therapeutic role of counselors is to assist clients in acquiring an understanding of both the external and internal forces that govern their relationships, thus providing clients with the skills and ability to define, assess, and correct their behaviors.

The foundation for assumption 3 is based upon a belief that clients can be empowered with an ability to define, assess, and renegotiate, where possible, dysfunctional and non-productive relationships. Empowerment can be accomplished by explaining and interpreting for the client those external factors that have negatively impacted relationships, as well as the ineffective adaptive mechanisms utilized by the client. The client's current behavior, via dysfunctional relationships, is explored and interpreted. The impact of American racism as an external factor governing individual relationships is addressed, as is the impact and effect of American racism on the client as well as the larger African American community. Racism is addressed not as an excuse to justify irresponsible behavior by the client, but as a contributing factor, in most cases, to the development of dysfunctional and nonproductive relationships.

CONCEPTS OF THE CULTURALLY SPECIFIC TREATMENT MODEL

The Culturally Specific Treatment Model was developed around ten fundamental concepts. Each concept is interrelated and provides a frame of reference for the treatment of African American clients.

Concept 1

The Culturally Specific Treatment Model requires counselors to be knowledgeable of the history, culture, and behavior patterns of African Americans from slavery to the present day.

Frame of Reference for Concept 1

It is not necessary for counselors to absorb over four hundred years of African American history. It is necessary, however, that counselors acquire a general understanding of the circumstances surrounding the development of different phases of African American history, as well as the cultural adaptations and coping mechanisms that were and are utilized by African Americans. There is no question that African American culture and history did not develop solely within the confines of America. A number of scholars, (Karenga, 1984; Heal, 1982; Dobson, 1981; and La Frances Rogers-Rose, 1980) have provided evidence of West Africa's cultural patterns that were retained during slavery and are reflected in the lifestyles of African Americans. However, because of the conditions and circumstances under which African Americans have had to live in America, West African cultural patterns and beliefs had to be modified and adapted to the American slave system. West African cultural patterns and beliefs are traceable in the language, music, dress, dance, and behavior patterns of African Americans. An understanding of these cultural characteristics and behavior patterns, as well as their historical development, is necessary for counselors to have when working with African American clients.

Concept 2

The Culturally Specific Treatment Model acknowledges that the history of African Americans is unique and unlike the history of other American ethnic groups; due to racism, attempts have been made to deny Africans Americans their right to life, liberty, and the pursuit of happiness, which is a primary source of their uniqueness.

Frame of Reference for Concept 2

Concept 2 emphasizes the uniqueness of African Americans history, which is well documented. It is a history of slavery, racism, exploitation, and racial oppression, a history in which human rights and equal opportunities have been systematically denied; it is a history of struggle, self-determination, courage, resilience, and survival. A history where African cultural values, patterns, beliefs, and behaviors were retained, refined, modified, and incorporated into the lifestyles of African Americans. The African American group is the only group of Americans, with the exception of the Native American, that did not migrate to America. Four hundred years of chattel slavery followed by constitutionally driven Jim Crow laws are two main sources of African Americans' uniqueness.

African Americans were held in chattel slavery from 1626 to 1865. The Dutch introduced slavery into the colony of New Netherland, the future New York and New Jersey, when the Dutch West India Company imported eleven Africans. The first slaves were used as a public workforce to clear land, row crop, and build roads, houses, and forts. By 1670, the American system of chattel slavery had begun to emerge, and North Carolina, South Carolina, New York, New Jersey, and Maryland mandated lifetime servitude for negro slaves. Between 1701 and 1760, slave traders brought 252,000 Africans into the American colonies. The majority of slaves lived and worked on the plantations of the southern colonies growing tobacco, rice, and long staple cotton. As the slave numbers increased, constitutional laws were established to enforce and control the slave system. Marriages between slaves and whites were illegal. Slaves could not testify in court, and slaves were classified as real estate—in other words, slaves were legally defined as property and therefore could be killed at will by their owner.

The uniqueness of African American history is also reflected in African Americans' use of alcoholic beverages. Counselors working with African American alcoholics must understand the history of alcohol use in, as well as its impact on and importance to, the African American community. The following areas must be understood and addressed during the treatment process: (1) cultural and social factors related to alcohol abuse and alcoholism; (2) drinking patterns and practices; and (3) cultural barriers that interfere with treatment. An essential aspect of this concept is the counselor's ability to understand, interpret, and incorporate each of the above elements into the treatment process.

Cultural and Social Factors related to Alcohol Abuse and Alcoholism among African Americans

A number of explanations and theories have been postulated for the high incidence of alcohol abuse and alcoholism among African Americans. The theory of biochemical or physiological deficiencies, as well as psychological and emotional maladaptation, have been postulated. According to this theory, alcoholism is caused by physiological elements and processes. Alcoholism results from metabolic deficiencies or genetic makeup, thereby predisposing certain individuals to the disease. Watts and Wright (1983), referencing Ward (1980), wrote that "adherents of this perspective argue that 1. Certain people are born with a body chemistry that makes them potential alcoholics, and 2. Long years of drinking may alter the biochemistry of some people, which in turn causes further heavy drinking or alcoholism." Though there are differences between these explanations in terms of the initial cause of alcoholism, they both suggest that the underlying cause of alcoholism is physiologically based.

The psychological or maladaptation theories of alcoholism employ psychoanalytic theories or other psychological theories to explain the cause of alcoholism. Proponents of this theory argue that alcoholism is the consequence of unresolved psychological conflicts that developed during early childhood and that those early childhood experiences have been repressed into the unconscious. The personality trait theory is closely related to the psychoanalytic theories. Alcoholism is explained as symptomatic of some underlying and distinct personality type that predisposes the person to excessive alcohol consumption. Studies report characteristics such as dependency, denial, depression, superficial sociability, emotional instability, suspiciousness, low tolerance for frustration, and chronic anxiety as occurring with high frequency among alcoholics.

Another explanation is the "operative behavior" theory. According to the proponents of this belief, alcohol is a means for reducing anxiety and stress related to social inequalities, hardships, and emotional problems. Proponents of this theory argue that alcoholism is a socially acquired behavior that is maintained by stimulus cues and social reinforcement contingencies. It is believed that excessive consumption of alcohol enables the alcoholics to avoid or escape from unpleasant, anxiety-producing situations. It is also believed that alcoholism develops and is sustained because it is reinforced by environmental influences that are outside of the person. According to this theory, a *reinforcer* is anything that increases the likelihood that the problem drinking will reoccur in the future. For example, the need for social approval from peers, friends, or relatives is an important positive reinforcer that in part perpetuates alcoholism. It allows alcohol abuse to continue because it wards off or removes negative feelings of unpleasantness and unwanted experiences; when this occurs, the drinking behavior is negatively reinforced. In essence, the earmark of alcoholism from the operative behavior perspective is that it is initiated and maintained by a combination of positive and negative social environmental reinforcers.

The Culturally Specific Treatment Model views alcoholism and other disorders as inappropriate adaptive or survival mechanisms cope with to the oppressive conditions under which African Americans have lived in

America. Alcohol has been the acceptable means to temporarily escape racism and the hardships of the environment for most African Americans. The use of alcohol in this manner has been an adaptive mechanism. For many, the ability to appropriately handle stress associated with racism and discrimination has been the end result of weekend drinking and celebration. Alcoholism occurs when African Americans are unable to develop appropriate adaptive or survival mechanisms in response to racism, discrimination, and social, economic, and/or political oppression. Alcoholism and other disorders also occur when African Americans are not able to master the skill of duality. The skill of duality is a primary adaptive technique that African Americans are forced to utilize in order to survive the conditions of racism. Duality is the ability to move back and forth between the white world and the black world, and/or between mainstream society and the African American community. African Americans who have mastered this technique are referred to as bicultural, marginal, nationalists, or integrationists. Those African Americans that do not master the duality skill are usually fixated either in mainstream America or within the African American group.

Drinking Patterns and Practices

It is believed by many African Americans that the current drinking patterns and practices of African Americans developed in response to economic and political powerlessness, psychological and sociological problems, victimization, and racial discrimination (Harper, 1976; King, 1987; and Kane, 1981). Proponents of this belief contend that the historical patterns of alcohol use and non-use by African Americans have played a significant part in influencing their current attitudes toward drinking. Additionally, it is believed that the mixed signals given to Africans by European Americans during slavery—some encouraging African Americans to drink and others discouraging African Americans' use of alcohol—has also contributed to a sense of ambivalence and confusion regarding whether or not to drink. African Americans, therefore, end up choosing one of two extremes: (1) to drink heavily or (2) not to drink at all. It has been established that the well-described patterns of contemporary African American drinking on weekends and on paydays is connected with the historically established patterns of drinking heavily in free times and drinking as a reward for work. African American drinking patterns and practices are also reflected in their culture and social institutions. The use of alcohol is reinforced by the lifestyles of many African Americans. It is viewed as a way of life. Celebration is an important concept among African Americans.

The tradition of celebration is an old one that characterizes an African legacy. African Americans make themselves feel good by engaging in activities that produce positive affective experiences. The cultural and social expectation, therefore, at social gatherings and festive occasions where alcohol is provided, is that everyone present will drink. The tolerance level for non-drinkers at these gatherings is low; however, heavy drinking and drunkenness are not only tolerated, but expected. Alcoholism, on the other hand, is seen as a problem as well as an indication that the person is not able to handle his/her liquor. Alcohol is an acceptable means by which African Americans make themselves feel good and escape the hardships and frustrations of being African Americans. Community-defined standards that determine what is appropriate alcohol use have not been established by African Americans for African Americans. Appropriate alcohol use or misuse was established during slavery. Therefore, the relationship between racism and substance abuse is no different from the relationship between racism and any other aspect of black life. The easy accessibility of liquor stores in low-income communities next to schools, churches, and homes not only contributes to the high rate of alcohol abuse and alcoholism among African Americans but also reinforces and perpetuates everyday racism.

Cultural Barriers to Treatment

Cultural barriers that interfere with the successful treatment of African Americans are usually not addressed during the treatment process. It is believed that conventional treatment methods and techniques are applicable to all clients, regardless of ethnic background. Not only do African Americans present themselves differently to treatment in terms of perceptions and lifestyles, but their expectations of treatment are usually different from those of the counselor. According to Wheeler (1977),

African Americans "come with a different set of expectations, including the assumption that the counselor must be an expert. Given the expert expectation, it is not unusual that black clients will ask their counselors to advise them and expect to receive this advice. It is also not unusual for a black client to ask very directly, 'What would you do if it were you with this problem?' To understand this, one must understand that, when potential black clients seek assistance from friends or relatives, they are seeking advice, or clarification and re-direction." For most African American clients, the issue of race will be a central theme in treatment. Their perception of race is directly related to their experiences. Poor housing, lack of education, unemployment, discrimination, the criminal justice system, and other legal problems may account for many of their problems. Most will blame the "the system or "the white man." Some will blame themselves; for others, no one is to blame. Counselors working with these clients must help them assess, interpret, and renegotiate their dysfunctional relationships, as well as those external forces that are impacting them. Counselors must introduce and teach clients effective adaptive skills and strategies aimed at modifying and/or manipulating those external systems that are negatively impacting them.

African American communication styles, language, and perceptions of time are additional barriers to treatment. Most African American clients will manifest a reluctance to self-disclose; consequently, they are closed and nonverbal in counseling sessions. African Americans as a group were brought up with the belief that "you do not discuss your personal business outside of the home or with strangers." There are many reasons for this belief; a common reason is family secrets. Family secrets may involve protecting family members who may be engaging in illegal activities. Family members know that if the activities are known, the security and safety of the family will be in jeopardy. Examples of some activities are having family members live in the home who are not on the lease, conducting business operations inside the home without a license, selling government food for money, selling bootlegged items and other sellable items without a peddler's license, and selling or buying stolen items. There are other family secrets that are more damaging to the family that are not shared.

African Americans' use of language is another reason for little or no communication between counselor and client. Whenever an African American client feels that he or she is unable to effectively communicate with the counselor, and/or if the client believes that the counselor is unable to understand the problems from the client's frame of reference, effective treatment will not occur. Another barrier to treatment is the concept of time. Most African American clients will not return to treatment if they have to wait a number of days for an appointment or if there is a delay in the start-up of treatment. According to Block (1984), African American "active" style demands that one do something right away, and if treatment is not available within a relatively short period of time, another method of dealing with the problems will be sought. Block (1984) states that often this dynamic is mistakenly viewed as "patient resistance."

Tardiness and missed appointments are other variables that are associated with resistance to treatment. Time is a major concept in the treatment process. However, the cultural difference in regard to time is not considered in treatment. African American clients' expectations and view of linear time will probably differ from those of counselors. Within the African American community, there is a phase called "colored people time." This phase was developed because most events facilitated by African Americans do not start on time. Punctuality as a concept in and of itself is not valued by the African American community. According to Jones and Black (1984), "For more than three centuries, African Americans have not been able to control their future. Therefore, linear time has been less relevant. The surface aspects of time would suggest that the interpretation of behavior in the context of time, such as punctuality, may not have comparable meaning for African American clients. That is, the temporal unit itself may mean something different to African American clients so time-based notions of resistance may be less applicable." Because of the cultural differences in the perception of time and the fact that most African American clients will be entering treatment for the first time and will be unfamiliar with the rules that govern time, instructions regarding time as well as the rationale and expectations of clients regarding time should be provided during the first interview.

Concept 3

Culturally Specific Treatment views alcoholism and alcohol abuse as the number one health and social problem within African American communities.

Frame of Reference for Concept 3

Concept 3 addresses the health and social problem associated with substance use disorders. The problem of alcoholism and drug addiction is a serious health and social problem for African Americans. It is associated with physical illness and mental disorders, crime, suicide, accidents, and other personal and social problems. Alcohol abuse is the number one health and social problem, historically ignored by African Americans. The use and abuse of alcohol by African Americans has increased over 86 percent since the 1970s. After heart disease and cancer, alcoholism is the number one killer of African Americans. We have, for instance, twelve times more cirrhosis of the liver among urban black males under the age of thirty-five years than for any comparable age group. Alcoholism is said to shorten the lifespan of African Americans by fifteen years. According to the United States Life Expectancy 2017 report, African Americans' life expectancy is 72.29 percent, compared to 76.60 percent for European Americans. Alcoholism and alcohol abuse are implicated in cancer and 88 percent of all other medical problems. Sixty-five percent of all hospital beds are occupied by persons with alcoholism as a secondary diagnosis. Alcoholism and/or alcohol abuse have been implicated clearly in the following areas: 61 percent of all job absenteeism, 84 percent of all traffic deaths, 34 percent of all suicides, 65 percent of all family violence, 70 percent of all violent crimes, 90 percent of all stabling, 80 percent of all arrests for crimes with weapons, and 50 percent of all homicides (King, 1981). King (1983) further states that "the problem of alcoholism has not yet been fully legitimized in the black community so as to allow community-defined standards, folkways, and mores on the subject of drinking. What we see rather is an increasing use of alcohol at an earlier age by youth and a growing intensity by women."

African American alcoholics and drug addicts in many cases also have an undiagnosed mental illness. After being diagnosed, these clients are classified as either dually-diagnosed or MISA (Mentally Ill Substance Abusers). However, when comparing alcohol abuse, alcoholism, and drug addiction with mental health, one would find that a definition for mental health, as well as the identification and treatment of psychological problems, is a more complex process than it is for substance use disorders. For example, in most cases of mental illness, there is not a deterioration in body organs and systems that can be identified; the exception to this are mental disorders that are due to a general medical condition. Additionally, with most mental disorders, there is not a single prescription for recovery that is applicable for everyone who may be suffering from the same disorder; therefore, the medical model of disease cannot be uniformly applied to the substance use disorder population. Due to generations of institutionalized racism, poverty, and feelings of helplessness and hopelessness, life chances and opportunities for many African Americans have be obstructed by mental illness, alcohol abuse, alcoholism, and drug addiction.

Concept 4

Culturally Specific Treatment views the use of alcohol by African Americans primarily as a means of escape from personal problems, poverty, racism, alienation, discrimination, and other injustices.

Frame of Reference for Concept 4

During slavery, alcohol was given to African American slaves for two primary reasons: (1) to combat slave insurrections, and (2) to reward slaves for hard work and obedience. African Americans perceived the use of, and consequently used, alcohol as a means of temporary relief from the hardships of slavery. Following slavery and subsequent periods of history, the use of alcohol by African Americans was primarily a means of coping with as well as an escape from their environmental conditions. Harper (1977) states, "Social factors associated with problem drinking among urban working class include poverty background, early failure, and family instability." Davis (1973) reports that the "changes from rural to urban life for blacks brought marked changes in the black man's behavior patterns. These changes are very much in evidence in his family structure and relationships. For a large number of blacks, the consumption of cheap wines, beers, and bathtub gin became a way of coping with basic changes in their environment." Kane (1981) asserts that "alcohol provides relief or escape from the many frustrations of being black in America. Racism seems the best term for the core problem underlying these frustrations." The role of racism in the development of alcohol problems among blacks is recognized by several authors, while the influence of racism on the drinking of blacks living in deprivation is obvious. Davis (1973) points out that racism stresses middle- and upper-class blacks as well often contributing to excessive alcohol consumption among them. Expressions of racism cited in the alcoholism literature include poverty and urban ghetto living, unemployment and underemployment, and the scarcity of alcoholism treatment resources for poor blacks (Davis, 1973).

Concept 5

Culturally Specific Treatment maintains that African American alcoholics and drug addicts suffer a double stigma: (1) they are African Americans, and (2) they have substance use disorder.

Frame of Reference for Concept 5

Wright (1984) states, "Black alcoholics suffer a kind of double indemnity in American society, for they are both black and alcoholic To be either has historically been problematic and somewhat less than popular within the American societal fabric." Within America, alcoholics are generally viewed as either drunks or sinners. There are many, however, who believe alcoholics have a health problem and/or disease. The African American alcoholic and drug addict however, is blamed not only for his or her addiction but also for the conditions that contribute to excessive drinking and drug usage—i.e., the oppressed person is blamed for his or her oppression. Race-related stress and everyday racism coupled with an external locus of control, however, are major contributors to the high incidence of alcoholism and drug addiction among African Americans. Being stigmatized as less than their white counterparts, being seen as criminal, and being denied the right to life, liberty, and happiness are also variables that can be linked to the abuse of alcohol and drugs by many African Americans. The double indemnity stigma is an area that counselors must re-educate clients around, as well as empower them to believe in their own humanity, capabilities, and rights as human beings.

Concept 6

Culturally Specific Treatment does not adhere to the disease concept of alcoholism. In Culturally Specific Treatment, the behavioral aspects of alcoholism are the central themes in the treatment process, thereby placing the responsibility for changing negative behaviors and dysfunctional relationships on the client.

Frame of Reference for Concept 6

The National Council on Alcoholism defines alcoholism as "a chronic progressive and potentially fatal disease. It is characterized by tolerance, physical dependency, and pathological organ changes, all of which are the direct or indirect consequences of the alcohol-infested. All symptoms of alcoholism result from physical adaptation to alcohol and are to be accounted for in terms of the progressive effects of alcohol on the body and never from the character or personality of the victim of that adaptation. Therefore, the only way to treat an alcoholic is as a person who has unwittingly, progressively poisoned himself with a chemical that causes insanity, death, or both." The National Council on Alcoholism further indicates that behavior changes in alcoholics are the result of the progressive adaptation of the body to the toxic effects of alcohol. Therefore, psychosocial systems must be viewed in relation to the effect of alcohol on the body of the alcoholic. The notion of a disease places responsibility for the alcoholic's behavior on the alcohol, absolving the alcoholic of any responsibility for consciously contracting the disease. *Abscess* (1981–1982) a journal published by the Michigan chapter of the National Black Alcoholism Council, states that the disease concept of alcoholism has found much acceptance among European Americans. African American alcoholics, however, generally do not accept the disease concept as an explanation for their alcoholism. Most African Americans perceive alcoholism as a state of drunkenness and/or as a means of making it through the day, *not as a disease.* The basis for the above belief can be found in the culture of African Americans, primarily in the area of spirituality.

African Americans are spiritual people; therefore, the belief system of many African Americans includes the concept of spiritualism. Spiritualism is a belief that all things, living or dead, influence each other and that there is no separation between the body, mind, and spirit. It is a belief that external forces—i.e., God, spirits, or other deities—control man's destiny. Good health is perceived as being in harmony with nature, but outside of man's control. Poor health and illness, on the other hand, are perceived as being in disharmony with nature, and also out of man's control. Many African Americans believe that the state of their life and health is predetermined by forces outside of their control. They are therefore not responsible for their illnesses and/or diseases. Alcoholism does not fit into the above belief system. Drinking alcohol is viewed as a conscious act, something that is within the control of the individual. The alcoholic is therefore responsible for his condition as well as his behavior. Most African Americans do not perceive alcoholism as a disease. Cancer, a liver disorder, a heart disease, or a stroke are all viewed as diseases or illnesses that are beyond the control of man; alcohol use is not.

Concept 7

Culturally Specific Treatment is based upon a belief that African Americans have emerged from a series of complex relationships: slavery, racism, discrimination, oppression, and poverty.

Frame of Reference for Concept 7

The relationship that has historically existed between African Americans and European Americans is one of racism and racial oppression. Because of the nature of this relationship, the majority of African Americans have been concentrated in lower socioeconomic groups, where most life experiences consist of poverty, hopelessness, oppression, and despair. The life experiences of some African Americans, however, do not consist of poverty, hopelessness, or despair—i.e., those of the middle and upper classes. The African American middle and upper classes have reached a level of economic security within America. They have, nevertheless, been systematically denied the equality, respect, acceptance, opportunity, and recognition that is extended to their European American counterparts. The disparity that exists between African Americans and European Americans is clearly reflected in income levels.

In 2015, the income levels of both the African American middle and upper classes were below those of their European American counterparts. The fact that the majority of African Americans are concentrated in the lower middle class (sales-clerical) is the reason given to account for the two-thousand-dollar deficit that is reported for this class as a whole. The average income for lower-middle-class African Americans was reported as $5,500 below the requirement for the middle-class living standards. It has been documented that a significantly larger percentage of middle-class African Americans than whites lack the income required to live up to the standard of the middle class as a whole, nor have upper-class blacks caught up with their white counterparts relative to income. The average income for upper-middle-class whites exceeds that of African Americans by almost two thousand dollars. Even though many African Americans have reached middle- and upper-class status within the last decade, they have not been as successful as their European American counterparts in the accumulation of wealth. Additionally, because the middle and upper classes of African Americans have more debt and less disposable income after expenses, their position within these classes is less secure. Most are living from one paycheck to the next.

Many African Americans in the middle and upper classes believe they have made it economically and are confident that they will keep what they have acquired; but because racism is such a salient factor in black-white relationships, many African Americans in these groups never receive the recognition or opportunities they deserve. They never know, for example, whether they are passed over for promotion and salary increases because of their race or because of other factors. The standards, behaviors, and lifestyles of middle- and upper-class African Americans have emerged as a consequence of racial segregation and discrimination, and even though they may have achieved a certain status within the African American community, within European America, disparities continue to exist in most areas of their lives.

Concept 8

Culturally Specific Treatment requires that treatment be holistic, addressing the relationships of the whole person i.e., physical/biological relationships, political/economic relationships, social/interpersonal relationships, and traditional/spiritual relationships.

Frame of Reference for Concept 8

Culturally Specific Treatment requires holistic treatment that addresses the relationships of the whole person; the relationship areas are physical/biological relationships, political/economic relationships, social/interpersonal relationships, and traditional/spiritual relationships. The Culturally Specific Treatment Model incorporates concepts from the Fanon Model of "The Person and Family in Society," which was presented by Dr. .Lewis King at the National Black Alcohol Council conference in 1984.

Physical/Biological Relationships: Physical/biological relationships are those relationships that African American clients have with their physical world. A part of a person's essence, according to Dr. King, is defined by the circumstances surrounding his or her world and/or physical space. Physical/biological relationships are defined, therefore, as those circumstances associated with clients' physical and psychological well-being, such as food, shelter, clothing, security, and mental and physical health. Counselors working with African American clients must identify, interpret, and integrate into the treatment process those physical/biological relationships that are dysfunctional and do not contribute to the growth, development, and well-being of clients.

Political/Economic Relationships: Political/economic relationships are those relationships that clients have with institutions within and outside of their communities. An institution is defined as a power base that is devoted to a special type of work. Institutions have the ability and the authority to influence the behavior of people. In political/economic relationships, focus is placed on the everyday institutions that are or should be impacting the lives of clients, for example, educational institutions, banks, police, department stores, grocery stores, transportation systems, social service agencies, employment agencies, the legal system, jails, prisons, jobs, and unions. Counselors working with clients must help them understand the role and power that institutions have on their lives as well as to teach them skills and approaches they can use to achieve a win-win situation when interacting with institutions inside and outside of their communities.

Social/Interpersonal Relationships: Social/interpersonal relationships are relationships that clients have with significant others, as well as interpersonal relationships in general. In social/interpersonal relationships, emphasis is placed upon understanding the daily relationships that clients have with people. In social/interpersonal relationships, focus is also placed upon identifying problems clients may have around the establishment of intimacy. Intimacy is defined as the ability to become vulnerable and to disclose pain to others without feeling judged. Counselors working with African American clients must educate them on the meaning of vulnerability and social connectedness, as well as assisting them in reconnecting with their family, friends, and the community.

Traditional/Spiritual Relationships: Traditional/spiritual relationships are those relationships that are associated with the customs, traditions, belief, and history of clients. In traditional/spiritual relationships, focus is placed upon clients' belief and value systems, as well as, their understanding of self. Counselors working with African American clients must understand and interpret for clients the relationships between their belief systems, their race, and their present problems. The restoring of personal control and efficacy, as well as assisting them in understanding their destiny and where they can fit, become primary goals.

Concept 9

The Culturally Specific Treatment Model maintains that treatment must teach new life skills that enable clients to renegotiate and change, where possible, relationships that are toxic and non-productive.

Frame of Reference for Concept 9

Concept 9's focus is on teaching clients new life skills. New skills are taught from a frame of reference that supports the belief that "all relationships are continuous and interrelated." The four primary relationship areas upon which the model is based are physical/biological relationships, political/economic relationships, social/interpersonal relationships, and traditional/spiritual relationships. Most traditional treatment approaches emphasize the fact that counselors should not advise or teach clients. Clients must instead make their own decisions and work through their problems by self-disclosure, free association, and the use of abstractions. If these approaches are used with African American clients, however, most will withdraw from the treatment process. According to Wheeler (1977) and Wash (1988), African American clients expect a more active, advice-giving counselor— someone who understands their problems, shares opinions, and gives directions. Counselors working with African American clients must teach them how to change their dysfunctional and non-productive relationships, as well as develop new life skills. Counselors must, therefore, ask the following questions regarding client's relationships: (1) What powers do clients have in each of their relationships? (2) Which relationships are toxic/dysfunctional? In order to answer the above questions, counselors must help clients understand both the internal and external conditions that are operating, as well as the factors that are governing each of the relationship areas.

Concept 10

Culturally Specific Treatment requires that counselors re-examine and re-interpret African Americans' response to traditional treatment models and that counselors learn and understand the different communication styles of African Americans.

Frame of Reference for Concept 10

The treatment approaches and strategies currently utilized within the fields of substance abuse and mental health were not designed to address the cultural differences of African Americans. According to Kochman (1981) and Wash (1988), cultural differences are generally ignored in the area of client-counselor communications. One reason for this deficiency is that cultural differences play a covert role in the communication process. Another reason is because both African Americans and European Americans assume that they share a system of beliefs and are operating according to identical speech and cultural conversation, which is not the case. White, middle-class standards are used as the basis for developing counseling techniques, strategies, and models. Most African American clients do not fit these standards. Their problems are, nonetheless, assessed within the context of these standards.

Culturally specific treatment is based upon the assumption that treatment strategies and approaches must reflect the history and cultural characteristics of African Americans. African Americans perception regarding eye contact, touch, time language, social distance, and other behavior patterns must be understood by counselors and incorporated into the treatment process. The counselor must abandon those principles and techniques of counseling that do not reflect the behavior and communication styles of African Americans. An example of this is eye contact. When utilizing traditional counseling techniques, counselors have been taught that eye contact is a variable that will determine whether or not a client is engaged in the counseling session. The lack of eye contact, by a client, is an indication that the client is not interested in the treatment process. If the above description of eye contact is applied blindly to African American clients, incorrect conclusions may result. Within the African American culture, eye contact is generally perceived as a dare or challenge. African American children are taught that they are not to look or stare directly in the eyes of their parents or other adults in authority. Those children caught having eye contact are accused of either rolling their eyes or challenging the authority of their parents or other adults.

In addition to the foregoing cultural variables regarding eye contact, African Americans were taught not to have eye contact with European Americans. There are numerous cases of lynching and beating of African Americans by European Americans as a result of eye contact or "eyeballing" at European American women and/or challenging the authority of European American men. Emmitt Till, an African American teenager who was visiting relatives in Money, Mississippi, is such as example. Emmitt Till was dragged from his relatives' home late at night, beaten, and killed by European American men. He was accused of staring and whistling at the store owner's wife. It was only after the Black Power and Civil Rights Movements of the 1960s and 70s that African Americans has been allowed to look European Americans in their eyes without possible repercussions or death. However, there are many African Americans, due to cultural carry-over, that still will not look European Americans in the eye for fear of repercussion or death.

In traditional counseling approaches, the use of touch and social distance are also variables that counselors use to engage clients in treatment, as well as a means by which counselors communicate empathy and understanding of their clients. The cultural interpretation of these variables, by African American clients also has not been incorporated into the treatment process. It is imperative that counselors working with African American clients understand, however, how social distance and touch are viewed. Unlike European Americans, an appropriate social distance for African Americans is an "arm length" away for communications. For most European Americans, however, an appropriate social distance, for face-to-face communication, is the length of one hand. If counselors attempt to engage African American clients closer than the prescribed social distance, clients will physically withdraw by moving backward until their comfort levels are reached.

Touch is a treatment technique that is used by counselors to engage clients in treatment and to show empathy and understanding. This is done by touching clients' hands, arms, shoulders. Touch as a treatment technique with African American clients, however, may be inappropriate based upon cultural differences and expectations. African Americans communicate through touch and gestures, and touch, for most African Americans, signifies familiarity and intimacy; only those persons who know them well or whom they trust are expected to touch them. Consequently, African American clients will perceive touching by a counselor early in the treatment process as improper and intrusive. They may interpret the touch not as a helping technique, but as an indicator of disrespect.

SECTION II

A MOVEMENT FROM CULTURALLY SPECIFIC TREATMENT TO MULTICULTURALISM

Culturally Specific Treatment as a viable treatment modality was embraced by the substance abuse and mental health fields during the latter part of the 1970s and the 1980s. Authors such as Sue, Sue, and Sue (1977) and Wash (1988) wrote articles and published books on the importance of culture in the treatment of minorities. It was believed that a more positive treatment outcome would result if focus was placed on cultural variables, such as beliefs, values, identity, communication patterns, levels of acculturation, language, religion, spirituality, and lifestyles. However, during the mid-1990s, a growing trend toward replacing culturally specific treatment approaches with multiculturalism was developing. As indicated earlier, it was during the late 1970s and the 1980s that many African American health providers begin advocating for and developing culturally specific treatment models and theories (Wash, 1988). While culturally specific treatment models and theories were initially designed to address the unique needs of African Americans, it was from this effort that other minority groups began to raise their issues. However, once the focus was taken off African Americans and was expanded to include other classified minorities, attention was taken off the history and culture of African Americans and more attention was given to the needs of other classified minority groups, such as Hispanics, Asians, and women. In order to address the needs of these groups, different terminologies emerged, such as *cultural diversity* and *multiculturalism*.

Multiculturalism blossomed during the 1990s. A proliferation of articles and studies were published regarding cultural diversity, multicultural counseling, and ethnic and racial identity. The American Psychological Association, or APA, for example, mandated training in cultural diversity, cultural sensitivity, and cultural awareness. Although cross-cultural proponents of multiculturalism are cognitive of cultural differences, and while multicultural psychology provides a cultural perspective, the frame of reference for analysis, interpretation, and conceptualization of human behavior is Eurocentric (Moses-Robinson, 2002). In addition to the APA, other professionals from diverse cultural and ethnic backgrounds began advancing the notion of multicultural treatment, thereby discounting culturally specific treatment. It was the general belief that all that was needed was an understanding that there are cultural differences and that traditional models and techniques could be modified to address the treatment needs of all clients. Additionally, some of these groups also believed that minorities had more in common with European Americans than they had differences; therefore, they continued advocating for multiculturalism and cultural diversity models and not culturally specific models.

Another underlying assumption of multiculturalism is that all minority groups have both strengths and limitations, and rather than being viewed as deficient, differences between groups are viewed simply as different. Even with the above definition, there is still an underlying theme that African Americans lack the necessary skills needed to assimilate. Assimilation for minorities groups whose history and cultures are intact have more to do with the dominant group accepting and accommodating differences in either language and/or levels of acculturation. Unlike African Americans, who were captured and brought to America as slaves, all other minority groups immigrated either legally or illegally to America with a goal of assimilation.

A sidebar of multiculturalism is being culturally competent. *Culturally competent* can be defined as accepting and respecting cultural differences. Being culturally competent also means being culturally sensitive. Understanding ethnic group differences in the ways that they communicate, as well as their customs, traditions, rituals, and belief systems can reflect cultural sensitivity. Cultural competence also operates from the notion that if one is knowledgeable about and accepting of the fact that there are culture differences, that is all that is needed for one to be culturally sensitive. However, if the above information is not integrated into the history and culture of the minority group member, effective treatment outcomes will not occur. Given the above description, the multicultural thrust appears to be revisiting the call for assimilation into American life that was prevalent during the middle half of the twentieth century. Assimilation into the values and lifestyles of European Americans was one of the goals of many minority immigrants who migrated to America. The assimilation process for these groups usually takes form during the second generation and is solidified by the third generation. Assimilation for African Americans has never been an option or a goal.

It was not surprising that during the time that other ethnic groups were assimilating into America and African American psychologists and health professionals were defining and developing theories and models from a culturally specific perspective, the inferiority model was raised by European American social sciences as a reason why African Americans could never be assimilated into America. The inferiority model reemerged during the last decade of the twentieth century with the publication of Murray and Herrnstein's book *The Bell Curve*. Even though the book was discredited by many scholars and the authors were called racists, the book reinforced a belief held by many European Americans regarding the intelligence and abilities of African Americans.

The Bell Curve essentially states that African Americans, on the average, are intellectually inferior to whites and that given the low IQ of African Americans, it is unfair to expect them to compete on equal grounds with European Americans. The authors also contend that the low IQ of African Americans is due to genetic inheritance and therefore it is permanent. The authors' position is that because low IQ begets low IQ, African Americans will remain in the lower classes, which are inundated with social problems, such as crime, poverty, homelessness, unemployment, illiteracy, and teenage pregnancy. Another assumption of the book is that given the low IQ of African Americans, programs such as Head Start and affirmative action are inappropriate because they would put African Americans into positions that should be reserved for the qualified, i.e., European Americans.

Many African Americans believe that there is an inherent danger in the growing acceptance of multicultural and cultural diversity models. They believe that as other ethnically and culturally diverse groups gain prominence in American society, their concerns will exert influence on the counseling and other professional fields and the unique needs of African Americans, who served as the original source for multicultural notions, will be in jeopardy of becoming lost within this new discipline.

CHAPTER 1

African-Centered Worldview

An African-centered worldview is defined as the conceptual and ideological framework derived from African cosmology (which asserts that the origin and the development of the universe began in Africa). It also asserts that African reality, history, culture, and philosophy are at the center of the universe for analysis, interpretation, and understanding of human nature (Kambon, 1990, and Moses Robinson, 2002).

African-centered treatment operates from an African-centered worldview, and it is the foundation of the Culturally Specific Treatment Model. It is a worldview that operates from the premise that there is an authentic African identity and that there exists an oneness of being between Africans in Africa and Africans throughout the diaspora. An African-centered worldview does not distinguish the self, or the *I*, from the collective, mainly the *we*. The phrase "I am because we are" is an example of an African-centered worldview.

The African-centered worldview places Africa at the foundation of life. It is a belief that African Americans are of African descent and operates from the principle that we Africans are one people. It is also an ideology that places African Americans at its intellectual center and uses black culture as the normative focus. For example, African Americans and Africans are viewed as the authorities and leaders in developing treatment models, approaches, and techniques for the assessment and treatment of African American and African clients. The African-centered worldview begins with a holistic conception of the human condition. For example interventions are based on the belief that optimal health is a balance between emotional, cognitive, personal, spiritual, and physical health and that therapeutic treatment services are needed whenever deficits exist in one or more of these areas (holistic approach).

An African-centered worldview provides African American scholars and professionals a blueprint for developing new definitions of who we are and who we should be as a people. It consists of adopting positions that includes social and political advocacy, as well as the incorporating of the African-centered worldview into the socialization, rearing, and education of African American children. It is a belief that until Africans within and outside of the United States are free from oppression, racism, and discrimination, the challenges and struggles for human rights will continue. The African-centered worldview also operates from a belief that all life is continuous and therefore can be understood and defined in terms of four interrelated relationship areas: physical/biological, traditional/spiritual, political/economic, and social/interpersonal. The assumption is that problems develop because one or more of the above relationship areas are diseased.

Diseased is defined here simply as having toxic and unfavorable environmental factors that have negatively impacted one's ability to grow and thrive in each of the relationship areas. A primary goal of treatment, therefore, is to empower clients with the ability to establish healthy relationships. During treatment, clients are able to acquire self- and group understanding, as well as regain a belief in their own self-worth via African American history and culture. Counselors assist clients in accomplishing the above task by defining and interpreting for them the relationship that exists between their present problems and African American history and culture.

CHAPTER 2

Culturally Specific Group Treatment Paradigm

Currently, there do not exist culturally specific evidence-based group treatment models that have been normed on lower-class African American clients with a substance use disorder. Evidence-based models, such as harm reduction and motivational interviewing, which are used for both individual and group treatment services, are generic at best. These evidence-based models do not reflect, take into account, or recognize the need for cultural specificity when treating African American clients. At best, they can be used as adjuncts to a culturally specific treatment model that has been developed for the treatment of African American clients.

In 2012, Dr. Eleanor Harris and Dr. Hattie Wash developed a culturally specific group treatment paradigm for working with lower-class African American clients. The model was applied to clients treated at EMAGES, Inc., where the primary client populations are African Americans enrolled in the outpatient substance abuse treatment program, the outpatient sex offender treatment program, and the outpatient acute mental health program.

EMAGES's clinical team provided evidence of successful outcomes of the culturally specific treatment model for both group and individual treatment services by citing treatment outcome data from two government funding agencies. Both group and individual treatment services incorporated the four treatment relationship areas of the Culturally Specific Treatment Model. As indicated earlier, the effectiveness of the model was evident in outcome data that was compiled by the Illinois Department of Human Services Division of Alcoholism and Substance Abuse (DASA) and by the Cook County Adult Probation and Social Service Departments of Illinois. DASA provide yearly outcome data for all agencies that it funds. Yearly performance reports cover many variables; however, only three variables are included: client engagement, client retention, and continuity of care. The above variables were chosen because they reflect the effectiveness of a program in the areas of return visits, engagement, and the use of ancillary services upon discharge. Outcomes measures for each of these variables are reflected below. Cook County Adult Probation and Cook County Social Service Departments collect yearly outcome data on the number of clients enrolled, types of discharge, and recidivism rates.

Using the data collected by the above funding agencies, EMAGES was able to demonstrate that the service delivery performance rates for both individual and group services improved yearly following the implementation of the Culturally Specific Group Model in 2012 as well as the Culturally Specific Treatment Model. Listed below are the state fiscal years (SFY) for 2013 to 2015. Listed below are the percentage of clients that were still engaged after four sessions and the percentages engaged after ten sessions or thirty days. The percentage of clients who were discharged with supportive services such as AA is also listed.

Level of engagement with at least four treatment sessions during the first thirty days of treatment:

EMAGES level of Engagement	Statewide Level of Engagement
SFY 2013 51.0%	SFY 2013 47.8%
SFY 2014 58.6%	SFY 2014 39.5%
SFY 2015 62.6%	SFY 2015 42.1%

Level of engagement with at least ten treatment sessions after the first thirty days of treatment:

EMAGES Level of Engagement

SFY 2013 58.5%

SFY 2014 55.2%

SFY 2015 71.3%

Statewide Level of Engagement

SFY 2013 25.2%

SFY 2014 14.0%

SFY 2015 21.4%

Percentage of clients discharged with Twelve-Step group participation and supportive services:

EMAGES Discharges		Statewide Discharges	
SFY 2013	50.5%	SFY 2013	77.7%
SFY 2014	64.3%	SFY 2014	77.2%
SFY 2015	54.3%	SFY 2015	78.2%

Current literature indicates that African Americans generally will not seek out treatment services. Several reasons have been cited for the under-usage of services, such as counselor variables, perception of a counselor's ethnicity, and therapists' counseling styles (Okonji, Jacques, Ososki, Joseph, and Pulos, Steven, 1996). Consequently, the level of engagement in most treatment settings is low for African Americans. African Americans tend to use emergency rooms and/or crisis intervention services instead of services from traditional outpatient treatment facilities. Those African Americans who do seek services from outpatient treatment facilities tend to discontinue treatment services after the first or second visit. Two main reasons are noted for early termination of African American clients. (1) Counselors are not of the same race. African American clients tend to prefer counselors from their race (Cross and Grim, 2016). (2) Counselors outside of the client's race are usually not able to understand the differences in language (for example, slang/and or Ebonics), as well as dress, mannerisms, emotional expression of feelings, and lifestyle differences. Additionally, African American clients may mistrust their counselors and refuse therefore to discuss personal business for fear of negative outcomes.

EMAGES's data on client retention also indicates that we have been able to engage and maintain clients in treatment. Our retention rate and successful discharge rates are both over 50 percent for the three years that the Culturally Specific Group Treatment Model has been implemented.

The average for the above three years is 56.3 percent, which indicates that more than half the clients admitted and successfully discharged were provided with referrals to Twelve-Step programs or other ancillary services. (http://.dhs.state.il.us/page.aspx, 2013, 2014, and 2015).

The data for Cook County Adult Probation and Social Service Departments also indicates good client retention rates, as well as a successful discharge rate. Reflected below are the number of clients enrolled during the three-year period, type of discharges, and the number of recidivist clients. Most of the clients in the sex offender treatment program are enrolled for one or more years; therefore, enrollment numbers each year are duplicated numbers. Even though the sample population for the sex offender program is low, the maximum number of clients in treatment at any given time for the three-year period is eighteen. The retention rate for the eighteen clients is high, and the recidivism rate is low. All clients that were enrolled in FY 2015 were still enrolled December 31, 2016. All clients were also in the program for one or more years.

# Clients Enrolled	# Clients Discharged	Type of Discharge	# of Recidivists
FY 2013	FY 2013	FY 2013	FY 2013
15	2	1 Successful	3
		1 Death	
FY 2014	FY 2014	FY2014	FY 2014
18	3	3 Successful	1
FY 2015	FY 2015	FY 2015	FY 2015
16	0	0	0

Culturally Specific Group Treatment Model

The Culturally Specific Group Treatment Model consists of four phases: (1) a check-in phase; (2) a psycho-educational phase; (3) a clinical processing phase; and (4) a consultation phase. The clinical processing phase is where the four treatment relationship areas of the Culturally Specific Treatment Model are assessed, interpreted, and applied to the lives of the group participants. Each treatment phase is governed by overarching assumptions and guidelines.

Phase 1: Check-In Phase

Assumptions for the Check-In Phase

1. The majority of clients enrolled will be in group for the first time.
2. The expectations from the group of clients who have never been in a treatment setting will differ from those of the group facilitators.
3. The majority of clients will not be invested in the treatment process or open to change initially.
4. Clients who were unsuccessful in traditional treatment programs will see group treatment as a necessary evil.
5. Clients will have to understand the group process and group expectations before they can benefit from the group.
6. Some clients will be actively using alcohol or drugs and/or will be involved in the solicitation or transportation of drugs, and some will present with mental health issues.
7. Group facilitators are to be consistent, fair, and firm when implementing this phase of the treatment process.
8. The majority of clients will currently be involved with the criminal justice system and will initially see EMAGES as an extension of that system.
9. Group facilitators serve as role models relative to time, dress, behavior, and professionalism both within and outside of the group.
10. Group facilitators have written group rules that are discussed in group and given to each group member upon admission. Group rules are discussed each time a new member enters the group.

Guidelines for Implementation of the Check-In Phase

1. Group starts on time, regardless of how many clients are present.
2. Staff, consultants, and students assigned to groups are present at the start and remain a part of the group until the group is ended and the wrap-up is completed.
3. All fees are collected before the start of the group.
4. The duration of the check-in phase is fifteen minutes.

5. Group members can check in the group by stating their names, length of time in treatment, drug of choice, length of time they have been alcohol- or drug-free and/or free from drug involvement, and how they have been since the last group session. Struggles with sobriety and other pertinent issues are shared during this time. (Note: no processing is to take place doing this phase). If this is an acute mental health group and/or a sex offender group, the check-in process is the same. The focus, however, for the sex offender clients is on community safety and compliance with the conditions of their court supervision. Focus for mental health clients is on symptom reduction, medication compliance, if applicable, and stabilization.

Phase 2: Psycho-Educational Phase

Assumptions of the Psycho-Educational Phase

1. Psycho-education is a key component for the stabilization and reintegration of clients back into their communities.
2. Clients in general will not have an understanding of and will not be able to acknowledge the impact that their addictions, sex offending behaviors, or mental illness have had on themselves, their families, or their communities.
3. Educational topics on African American history, lifestyles, and culture, as well as specific topics on addiction and mental illness, will assist clients in moving closer to understanding the need for abstinence and toward living a productive life style.
4. Information on resources within and outside their communities assists clients in their reintegration back into the community by providing them with options and services that they can utilize.
5. Psycho-education is where the change process begins if clients are willing to share experiences and connect with group members with the same or similar life experiences.
6. Psycho-education is designed to provide clients with strategies, techniques, and skills for managing and coping with symptoms,

addressing problems, and embracing a drug-free and non-offending lifestyle.

7. Staff and consultants are knowledgeable of the history and psychosocial development, as well as the political and economic status, of clients in their groups. They also have an understanding and have been trained on each of the culturally specific treatment relationship areas, thereby providing them with the foundation for the psycho-educational phase of treatment.

8. One key component of the psycho-educational phase is education on the role that alcohol and drugs have historically played in the lifestyles of African Americans, as well as the role that they are currently playing in their lives. Assisting clients in breaking the historical cycle of addiction and offending behaviors is a primary objective.

9. Staff and consultants are flexible team players who are open to new and innovative ways of providing treatment to African American clients.

Guidelines for Implementing the Psycho-Educational Phase

1. The psycho-educational phase is scheduled for thirty-five minutes and is devoted to specific topics.

2. The format for the psycho-educational phase is open, interactive and electric. Group input, sharing, and participation are key components.

3. Group facilitators are prepared for each session with psycho-educational topics.

4. Each session starts with the group facilitators briefly explaining the topic and reasons why that topic was chosen. Handouts and other materials related to the topic are available for the group at the beginning of group.

5. Specific topics on the current social, economic, and political status of African Americans, as well the history, culture, and adaptive mechanisms, both positive and negative, that have been and are used by African Americans to adapt to the conditions of discrimination and racism, are also introduced and discussed.

Some examples of group topics that can be used for the psycho-educational phase are listed below:

- History of alcoholism and drug use in the African American community.
- African Americans' drinking patterns from slavery to the present day.
- The relationship between alcohol/drug addiction and unemployment in the African American community.
- Employment options for African American sex offenders (if this is a sex offender group).
- History of heroin addiction in the African American community.
- The crack cocaine conspiracy in African American communities: fact or fiction?
- Value of gender and culturally specific self-help groups for African American clients.
- Impact of drug addiction, mental illness, and sex offences on the African American community. (Separate presentations are developed for each.)
- Self-employment: one option for clients in general, and specifically for clients with felony convictions.

Handouts and presentations on each of the above topics are used to discuss the topic not only from a broader African American perspective, but also from the clients' perspective. Education is designed to assist clients in understanding the role that they play as contributors to their problem, as well as providing them with corrective action steps that are available to them.

Below are examples of general psycho-social educational group topics that can also be used by group facilitators. Each topic can also be two clients.

- Alcohol and legal drugs
- Impact of alcohol on the body
- Cocaine and the effect on the body

- Understanding the differences between crack cocaine and powder cocaine
- Marijuana and its impact on the body
- Should marijuana be legalized? Pros and cons
- Heroin addiction
- Impact of addiction on families
- Prescription drug abuse and addiction

Phase 3: The Clinical Processing Phase

Assumptions of the Clinical Processing Phase

1. The clinical processing phase takes place during the last forty minutes of group.
2. A holistic approach that incorporates the culturally specific treatment relationship areas is used to assess problems and issues presented during group. The relationship areas are physical/biological, social/interpersonal, political/economic, and traditional/spiritual.
3. Counselors assist group members in identifying, assessing, and interpreting internal and external factors and stressors that contribute to the continuation of problems and/or issues.
4. Changing or renegotiating the role clients play in maintaining problematic relationships is addressed during the clinical processing phase.

Guidelines for Implementing the Clinical Processing Phase

1. Following the psycho-educational phase, a group facilitator will ask a group member to volunteer to apply one or more of the relationship areas to his or her life. The group member is asked to answer the following questions: (1) What role does he or she play in maintaining one or more problems identified in each of the relationship areas? (2) How has it affected his or her life? (3) What are the internal and external factors that maintain the role that is played? (4) What does he or she want to do, i.e., change the role

or renegotiate the role? Clients may only be able to address one of the questions and one relationship area during a group session.

2. During the course of treatment, each group member will be asked to address each of the above questions. Each group member is expected to assess all four relationship areas and discuss whether he will change or re-negotiate the role he plays in each of the relationship areas.

Phase 4: Consultation Phase

Assumptions of the Consultation Phase

1. The consultation phase occurs at the conclusion of the group. Consultation is where the group facilitators assess the group process and group members.
2. Feedback from group facilitators and student interns to each other allows them to better process group dynamics, and understand clients none responses, as well as to monitor changes that have occurred in clients' behaviors and cognitive understandings.
3. Consultation provides an arena for group facilitators to discuss differences in approaches and techniques, thereby eliminating conflicts that may negatively impact the group process.

Guidelines for Implementing the Consultation Phase

1. The consultation phase occurs at the conclusion of each group session and lasts from ten to thirty minutes.
2. Facilitators and students give their impression of the group process and provide suggestions and input for the next group session. It is during this time that differences of opinion, techniques, and approaches are discussed and resolved.

CHAPTER 3

Treatment Planning

The last section of the treatment model is the development of the Culturally Specific Treatment Plan. Four areas are covered in this section: (1) an overview of the Culturally Specific Treatment Plan; (2) a case history; (3) common problems that appear in each of the relationship areas; and (4) a sample treatment plan for the case study.

The Culturally Specific Treatment Plan is placed on a grid-shaped form. The counselor's role is to assist clients in identifying, prioritizing, and entering on the treatment plan problems that have developed as a result of the roles they have played in each of the relationship areas. Specific goals and objectives aimed at changing or renegotiating identified problems are developed and entered on the plan. *Goals* are defined as expected outcomes that clients expect to achieve from treatment. Both short- and long-term goals are developed. *Objectives* are the tasks that clients will complete in order to accomplish their goals. Both goals and objectives are written in "I" statements by the client; for example, a client's goal could be "I want to stop selling drugs." An objective for this goal could be "I will stop going to the corner where drugs are sold." The purpose for using "I" statements is to put the responsibility for completing goals and objectives on clients. The content of the treatment plan is tailored to the individual needs of each client. Both the counselor and client discuss, share, and agree on the content of the treatment plan. The end result is the establishment of a treatment plan that is realistic and attainable, maximizing the possibility of an effective treatment outcome by each client. The Culturally Specific

Treatment Plan is discussed and developed during the initial session and/ or during the beginning stage of treatment. The initial stage is where the clinical needs are assessed and treatment in initiated.

Steps for developing a Culturally Specific Treatment Plan are as follows:

The Identification of Dysfunctional/Problematic Relationships

The first step in completing the Culturally Specific Treatment Plan is to identify the major areas in which treatment is expected to have an impact. A question to ask a client is whether the problems are influenced by the client (internal), by the environment (external), or by a combination of the two. An assumption of the model is that problems will exist in each of the four relationship areas.

Treatment Goals

The second step is to develop measurable goals for each relationship area. During this step, a determination is made between the client and counselor as to whether the client needs to change or re-negotiate the role he or she plays in each of the relationship areas. For example, a goal in the physical/ biological relationship area may be "I want to stop smoking marijuana." The counselor's intervention for this goal will be to focus on assisting the client in changing the relationship that he or she has with marijuana. A primary action step for each goal is to assist clients in either changing or renegotiating the role they play in each of the relationship areas.

Objectives, Methods, Staff, and Target Dates for Completion

The third step is for the counselor and client to determine an action plan (objectives) for addressing problems in each of the relationship areas. For example, if the client states that he or she cannot control daily marijuana usage, the counselor and client will discuss action steps that the client can take to control usage, as well as consequences if the client fails. In this section, activities and methods needed to change or renegotiate the relationship that the client has with marijuana are identified and placed on the treatment plan. Responsible staff, timeframes, and completion dates for this goal and other goals on the treatment plan are identified.

The treatment plan is also designed to allow for a process of trial and error toward completion, as well as for the utilization of different intervention techniques. The treatment plan is the guide and foundation for establishing an effective treatment outcome. The fourth step is to list specific evaluation techniques that will allow the counselor and client to follow progress, review accomplishments, and modify the plan when needed.

Funding bodies may require that additional information be included on the treatment plan; for example, a diagnosis, the initiation and review dates for the plan, or the signature of the client, counselor, LPHA, or physician. An aftercare plan, as well as a need for consultation and/or referral services after discharge, are additional items that may be on a treatment plan.

Case History

Deloris is a thirty-four-year-old, dark-complexioned African American female. Deloris appears to be of above average intelligence; however, she had difficulties answering questions. It appeared as if she was self-conscious of her southern dialect and her frequent use of slang and profanity when expressing herself. Eye contact with the counselor was minimal. Her posture indicated that she was uncomfortable during the entire interview process. Deloris is the fourth child in a "sib ship" of seven. She was raised on the south side of Chicago by her mother. Her parents divorced when she was six. Her father visited the family yearly after he remarried and moved to another state. During her adolescence, Deloris was a "loner," a pattern that she carried into adulthood. Deloris completed high school and married her high school sweetheart shortly after graduation. Deloris saw marriage as the only way she could get away from her mother. She describes her mother as stern and distant. According to Deloris, she has never been able to talk to her mother. During her first two years of marriage, she worked as a file clerk. She quit this job prior to the birth of her first child. Deloris has been separated for six years from her husband of sixteen years. She has two daughters, fourteen and thirteen. Her daughters were, however, placed in the custody of her mother a year ago because of child neglect, which resulted from Deloris's drinking. The relationship, consequently, deteriorated drastically when Deloris's mother gained custody of her daughters. Deloris seldom visits the girls because of the poor relationship with her mother and because of daily drinking. According to Deloris, her mother refers to her as the "family drunk" and not a child of hers. She also states that Deloris is not fit to raise her children, not only because she is a drunk, but because she had two abortions within the last five years. When asked her feelings regarding her mother's statement, Deloris stated that she was the "black sheep" of the family. She also stated that "she thought it was wrong to have an abortion, but she could not afford any more children, so she did what she had to do."

Deloris started drinking at the age of sixteen. She states that drinking made her forget her problems. Deloris would drink on weekends with her boyfriend (current husband) and her brothers. During the first five years of marriage, her drinking progressed to weekend binges. The drinking started on Friday and continued to Sunday. Deloris's husband, who also drank heavily, told her that if she did not stop getting drunk, he would leave her. Deloris's husband stayed with her, however, for several more years.

According to Deloris, "he left because of my drinking and that other woman." After she separated from her husband, Deloris's binges progressed to daily drinking. She indicated that everything fell apart after the separation. Deloris would spend most of her day at the corner bar. She had a group of drinking buddies, mostly men. When she did not have enough money, the men would buy her drinks. Deloris states that she drank whenever her problems become unbearable, which was most of the time. Deloris indicated that while living with her husband, she only drank when he did. She stated, however, that she also drank whenever her husband blamed her for his problems. According to Deloris, her husband has never been able to secure a stable, good-paying job. He has always worked, but in unskilled and "dead end" jobs. "He always blamed me," stated Deloris, "whenever things don't go well for him. He comes home and dumps on me—always telling me how bad I am as a wife and that I don't know how to treat a man. He would say that it's the black woman that is keeping the black man down because she won't work with him. I don't know what to say to him, so I drink." Deloris states that her husband would drink with her most times, "but he stopped at a certain point. I would continue drinking until I passed out." Deloris's source of income is general assistance (GA). Most of her money is spent on alcohol. The child support payments that she receives from her husband are given directly to her mother. Deloris's living environment is a run-down apartment building, and her health is poor, but she does not see these as problems. Her only concerns, presently, are to stop drinking and to regain custody of her daughters.

SECTION III

COMMON PROBLEMS IN RELATIONSHIP AREAS

COMMON PROBLEMS WITH PHYSICAL/BIOLOGICAL RELATIONSHIPS

Alcohol and drug addiction or abuse
Blackouts, memory lapses, tremors, delirium tremens
Dental and vision problems
Depression, anxiety, phobia
Situational adjustment disorders
Fatigue, headaches, digestive problems
Psychotic and other mental health disorders
Suicide attempts or thoughts
Other medical and psychiatric problems
Unemployment, hustling
Being un-domiciled
Substandard housing, i.e., lack of water, gas, lights, etc.
No source of income

COMMON PROBLEMS WITH POLITICAL/ECONOMIC RELATIONSHIPS

Problems on job, job pressures
Inability to find or obtain employment
Money management, insufficient income
Credit problems, inability to pay bills
Gambling or other spending habits
Poor academic background
Lack of vacation
Lack of job skill training
Lack of GED or basic adult education
Inadequate housing or living arrangements
Problems with landlords and/or other tenants
Pending legal problems (criminal or civil)
History of incarceration
Problems with police
Street gang activities
Problems with the Department of Children and Family Services (DCFS)
Problems with other social service agencies
Transportation issues

COMMON PROBLEMS WITH SOCIAL/INTERPERSONAL RELATIONSHIPS

Problems with family members, such as inability to communicate
Problems with girlfriend, boyfriend, or significant other
Problems associated with sexual orientation
Inability to obtain and/or maintain friends
Inability to communicate openly with others
Blaming others for problems
Little or no tolerance for opinions of others
Feeling of inferiority or shyness
Inability to trust or confide in others

COMMON PROBLEMS
WITH TRADITIONAL/
SPIRITUAL RELATIONSHIPS

Belief/nonbelief in a higher power or God
Dissatisfaction with religious faith
Belief in voodoo or hoodoo
Inability to trust people inside or outside of the race
Inability to trust people inside or outside of socioeconomic class
Problems associated with abortion
Problems associated with birth control
Feelings of betrayal to family
Feelings of alienation
Feelings of injustice or being trapped
Low self-esteem
Low self-worth
Immersion in or aspiration to mainstream value system
Individualism, materialism

SECTION IV

CULTURALLY SPECIFIC TREATMENT PLAN FORM

CULTURALLY SPECIFIC TREATMENT PLAN FOR CASE STUDY

Client Name: Deloris
SS#: 331-33-5568
ID#: 000001-SD
Admission Date: 01/11/2098

DSM-V/ICD10 Diagnosis: F10.23
ITP Date: 01/11/2098 ITP Review
Date: 01/11/2099

Problem/ Relationship area Area	Problem in Client's Words	Goal in Client's Words	Objectives, Method, Frequency, Duration	Staff Providing Service	Target Date
Problem 1: Physical/ Biological Relationship Area	"I am addicted to alcohol."	"I want to stop using alcohol."	Admission note and review of progress while in detox	Primary counselor	Thirty days from admission

Problem 2: Physical/ Biological Relationship Area	"I am sad and unhappy all of the time."	"I think I need medicine to help me feel better."	a. Counselor will review medication for compliance and side effects per session b. Client will attend weekly MISA groups Sessions for one and a half hours per session c. Client will attend bimonthly individual sessions to assist her in identifying internal and external stressors that contribute to depression	Primary counselor and group facilitator	a. The first sixty days of treatment b. The duration of treatment c. The duration of treatment
Problem 3: Social/ Interpersonal Relationship Area	"I do not get along with my mother. She wants to control my life."	"I want to be able to talk with my mother."	a. Provide client with steps on effective communication skills b. # of skills acquired and used to improve communication	Primary counselor	a. Progress notes and homework assignments b. Homework assignment on skills acquired and implement

Problem 4: Social/ Interpersonal Relationship Area	"I do not have friends except for the ones that I drink with."	"I will develop personal relationships with people outside of my drinking environment."	a. Number of groups/activities attended b. Client reports on number of socialization activities attended c. Client will homework assignments on self-image and self-perception	a. Group and primary facilitators b. Primary counselor c. Number of homework assignments completed by client	a. The first sixty days of of treatment b. After thirty days of treatment c. Weekly beginning thirty days after treatment is initiated
Problem 5: Spiritual/ Traditional Relationship Area	"I feel guilty about having an abortion."	"I want to move forward without feeling shame or guilt." "I will assess, process and renegotiate my feelings around my abortion."	a. Review progress notes b. Copy of completed inventory c. Review of progress notes	a. Primary counselor b. Primary counselor c. Primary counselor	a. To begin the third month of treatment b. During third month of treatment c. To begin the third month of treatment
Problem 6: Spiritual/ Traditional Relationship Area	"I do not like myself. I have low self-esteem."	"I can improve my self-image and my self-esteem."	a. Review of progress notes related to personal appearance, self-esteem, and self-worth	a. Primary counselor	a. Will begin after she completes detox

Problem 7: Political/ Economic Relationship Area	"I do not know how to take care of my children without getting mad at them."	"I will successfully terminate from the Department of Children and Family Services (DCFS) court mandate."	a. Client will discuss her feelings following each scheduled visit with children	a. Primary counselor b. Primary counselor	a. During first ninety days of treatment b. Bi-monthly visits with children
Problem 8: Political/ Economic Relationship Area	"My children are in the system."	"I will regain custody of my children."	a. Case conferences and copy of corrective action plan b. Number of sessions held as well as progress notes describing mother/children interactions	a. Primary counselor b. Primary counselor	a. First sixty days of treatment b. After a reunification date has been established by DCFS
Problem 9: Physical/ Biological Relationship Area	"I am unable to take care of my children because I don't have a job."	"I will explore and assess vocational interest, money, and employment options."	a. Copy of the monthly budget plan	a. Primary counselor and client	a. Six months of successful treatment

SECTION V
CONCLUSION

CONCLUSION

The failure of traditional treatment approaches to effectively address the cultural characteristics, as well as the treatment needs, of African American clients can be cited as a reason why a large percentage of African American clients prematurely withdraw from treatment services. A culturally specific treatment model provides a frame of reference from which professionals working in the helping fields can begin to understand the history, norms, values, and cultural characteristics of African American clients and how they can incorporate these variables into the treatment process. The model presented here was initially designed for the treatment of African American alcoholics; however, because it has been used to address the above treatment variables, as well as the historical realities of lower-class African Americans, it has been applied to client populations in mental health and other treatment settings.

The Culturally Specific Treatment Model not only identifies clients' problems, but it also provides a frame of reference for understanding the historical realities of life for lower-class African Americans living in America from a cultural, economic, and political framework. The model is designed to empower clients with tools that enable them to live productive lives within a racist and hostile environment where life, liberty, and the pursuit of happiness have been blocked for many of them. A culturally specific approach is necessary also because the twenty-first century has not eliminated the race problem. Racism is still alive, and overt forms of racism reemerged in the United Stated in 2008 with the election of the first African American president. Methods were employed by European Americans who carried the slogan "Make America great again" to discredit, block, and dismantle every law and accomplishment that was made by President Obama during the two terms that he was in office.

Coupled with the movement to "make America great again" was the election of members of the Conservative Right to government, mass incarceration of African Americans, killings of African American boys and men by police, banning Muslims from entering the United States, and the reversal of laws like voting rights and affirmative action. The dismantling of the Affordable Health Care Act, also known as Obama care, became the new direction of the Conservative Right during the first six months of Trump's election as president of the United States in 2016.

The disenfranchisement of lower-class African Americans, coupled with a failing service delivery and health system, requires that treatment providers understand not only the treatment needs of clients but also those external factors that contribute to alcoholism, drug addiction, mental illness, and other addictive disorders. Unlike the disparity that exists between African Americans and European Americans in the areas of physical health and life expectancy, which is well documented, the disparity in mental health, substance abuse, and other addictive disorders has not been well documented relative to etiology and recovery. Mental illness and substance abuse disorders are unlike a physical illness, where a blood test, a CAT scan, or other medical procedures can be performed to acquire a diagnosis. Mental illness and addictive disorders require different types of interventions. Interventions for African American clients have to include techniques and models that incorporate the history, lifestyles, and psychosocial development of African Americans from slavery to present day, as well as an understanding of the political, social, and economic factors that reinforce racist policies and laws that are designed to keep African Americans outside of the mainstream of America.

It is hoped that the above Culturally Specific Treatment Model will provide a foundation for the development of additional models, approaches, and techniques that are culturally specific for African American clients—models that not only assist clients in understanding the effects that both internal and external factors have had on them, but are also designed to aid them in reaching their highest potential and possibilities as productive members of society.

BIBLIOGRAPHY

Akbar. Naim. (1984). Chains and images of psychological slavery. New Jersey: New Mind Publications.

Alexandra, M. (2010). The new jim crow: Mass incarceration in the age of colorblindness. New York: The New Press.

Baum, Dan. (1996). Smoke and mirrors: The war on drugs and the politics of failure. Boston: Boston Little, Brown and company.

Blauner, Robert. (1972). "Racism and culture," in Racial oppression in america. New York: Harper & Row.

Brisbane, F. L. & Womble, M. (1985). Treatment of black alcoholics' ed. New York: Harper and Row.

Broom, L. & Gleen, N. (1965). "Nationalism and gradualism" in Transformation of the negro. New York: Harper and Row.

Burgest, David R. (1981). "Theory on whites supremacy/black oppression" in Black Book Bulletin, volume 7, number 2.

Clark, Kenneth B. (1979). "The civil rights movement: Momentum and organization" in The negro american. United States: Beacon Paperback.

Davis, Fred T., Jr. (1973). "Alcoholism among american blacks" Unpublished paper Presented at the 1973 Annual Meeting Alcohol and drug problems of North America.

Dawkins, Marvin P. (1983). "Policy issues" in black alcoholism: Toward a comprehensive understanding, ed. by Watts, Thomas D, and Roosevelt Whites Jr. Springfield, Illinois: Charles C. Thomas Publisher.

Dobson, Jualynne. (1981). "Conceptualization of black families" in Black families. ed., McAdoo, Harriette, Pipes. Beverly Hills California: Sage Publications.

Drake, St. Clair. (1970). "The social and economic status of the negro in the united states" in The negro american. ed., by Parsons, Talcott and Kenneth Clark, United States: Beacon Paperback.

Franklin, John H. (1970). "The two world of race: A historical view of the negro" in The negro american. United States: Beacon Paperback.

Gary, Lawrence. (1981). Black men. Beverly Hills California: Sage Publication.

Goode-Cross, Karen Ann Grim. (2016). "An unspoken level of comfort": Black therapists' experience working with black clients. The Journal of Black Psychology, volume 42, number 1 February, Sage Publications.

Golden, James L. & Richard D. (1969). The rhetoric of back americans. Ohio: Charles E. Merrill Publishing Company.

Gordon, Winthrop D. (1969). "American attitudes toward the Negro (1550 – 1812)" in Whites over black. Baltimore, Maryland: Penguin Books Inc.

Hale, Janice E. (1982). Black children: their roots, culture and learning styles. Utah: Brigham Young University Press.

Harper, Fredrick D. (1983). "Alcohol use and alcoholism among black americans a review," in Black alcoholism: Toward a comprehensive understanding. ed. Watts, Thomas D, and Roosevelt Wright Jr., Springfield Illinois: Charles C. Thomas Publishers.

Headley, Dorothy Knox. (1985). "Spirituality: a tool in the assessment and Treatment of black alcoholics" in Treatment of black america, ed., by Brisbane Frances Larry. & Maxine Womble, New York: The Hawthorne Press.

http://www.dhs.state.il.us/page.aspx. DASA SFY 2013, 2014 & 2015 Provider performance report.

Jones, James, M. & Carolyn B. Block. (1984). "Black culture perspectives" The Clinical Psychologists, special spring issue.

Kane, Geoffrey. (1981). Inner city alcoholism: An ecological analysis and cross cultural study. New York: Human Sciences Press.

Karenga, M. (1982). Introduction to black studies. California: Kawaida Publication

Katz, Judy H. & Allen Ivy. (1977). "Whites america: the frontiers of racism awareness training." Personnel and Guidance Journal.

King, Lewis M. (1983). "Alcoholism studies regarding black americans-1977-1980." in Black alcoholism toward a comprehensive understanding. ed. Watts, Thomas D. and Roosevelt Wright, Jr. Springfield Illinois: Charles C. Thomas Publisher.

Knochman, Thomas. (1981). Black and whites styles in conflict. Chicago & London: The University of Chicago.

Landry, Bart. (1987). The middle class. United States: University of Chicago Press.

Murry, Charles A. Herrnstein, Richard. (1994). The bell curve. New York: Simon & Schuster.

National Black Alcoholism Council Michigan Chapter. (1981-1982). ABCESS black and sedation. Michigan State Chapter.

Okonji, Jacques, M.A., Ososkie, Joseph N. & Pulos, Steven. Preferred style and ethnicity of counselors by african american males. Journal of Black Psychology, Vol.22 No.3 August 1996. @The Association of Black Psychology.

Pinkney, A. (1984). The myth of black progress. Massachusetts: Cambridge University Press.

Rose-Rodgers, LaFrances. (1980). The black woman. ed. Beverly Hills California: Sage Publications.

Sue, Derald Wing. (1977). "Counseling the culturally different: A conceptual analysis" Personnel and Guidance Journal March.

Sweets, L. (1976). "The role of blacks in american history." in Black images of america, 1784-1870. Toronto: W.W. Norton Company, Inc.

Talcott, Parson, & Kenneth B. Clark. (1979). The negro american. United States: Beacon Paper Back.

Wash, H. (1988). Culture specific treatment: A model for the treatment of african americans alcoholics. Chicago, Illinois: Jetpro Graphics.

Watts, Thomas D. Roosevelt Wright Jr. (1983). Ecological factors in black alcoholism: Toward a comprehensive understanding. ed. by Watts, Thomas D. and Roosevelt Wright Jr., Springfield Illinois: Charles C. Thomas Publisher.

Wheeler, William. (1977). "Counseling from a cultural perspective." Trainee Resources Manual. Atlanta Georgia.

Wright, J. (1969). "Black capitalism: toward controlled development of black america." Negro Digest, New York: December.

Wright, Emma J. (1984). "Counseling from a cultural perspective requisition for working with black clients." Unpublished paper. Atlanta Georgia: Southwest Regional Support Center.

ABOUT THE AUTHOR

Bio of Dr. Hattie Wash

Dr. Hattie Wash is one of the leading authorities on the treatment of African American clients. In 1988, Dr. Wash developed and published a culturally specific model designed for the treatment of African American alcoholics. Her treatment model is currently used at EMAGES, Inc., and has been used at other substance abuse treatment agencies. Dr. Wash has presented the model at numerous workshops and seminars and has received a number of awards and certificates for her work with African American clients.

Dr. Wash has an extensive work history in the fields of substance abuse and mental health services. She began her professional career in 1973 as an administrative trainee with the State of Illinois Department of Mental Health. She was assigned to the Garfield Park Mental Health Center on the west side of Chicago. The year prior to her employment, she graduated from Governors State University with a master's degree in cultural studies, with emphasis on African American studies. Her goal at that time was to teach at one of the City Colleges of Chicago or at Chicago State University. Because there were no teaching opportunities available, she took a job with the State of Illinois as an administrative trainee.

After one year in the State's administrative trainee program, she was hired at Garfield Park Mental Health Center, one of three federally funded comprehensive mental health facilities in the city of Chicago. This facility later became the Bobby E. Wright Mental Health Center. Dr. Wash worked for Bobby Wright from 1973 to 1979.

After leaving the Bobby Wright Mental Health Center, Dr. Wash became the director of the Minority Economic Development Institute's outpatient substance abuse program. It was there where she began to see that the needs of African American clients addicted to alcohol were not being addressed. She joined the National Black Alcoholism Council and later become one of the founding members of the Illinois chapter of the National Black Alcoholism Council. She also served as president of the Illinois chapter for two terms.

After leaving the Minority Economic Development Institute, Dr. Wash took a job at BRASS foundation as the director of their outpatient substance abuse program. She was later promoted to director of clinical services for BRASS Foundation, who at that time had two outpatient methadone programs and a children and adolescent program, as well as MISA and outpatient substance abuse treatment programs for both men and women. Dr. Wash left BRASS in 1990 to work on her doctoral degree in clinical psychology. While at BRASS, Dr. Wash developed and published her Culturally Specific Treatment Model and continued to advocate for culturally specific treatment models at conferences and workshops both locally and nationally. It was also during this period that she got an opportunity to teach substance abuse courses at Harold Washington and Kennedy-King City Colleges and at Chicago State University.

In 1992, Dr. Wash incorporated EMAGES as a not-for-profit counseling and psychological services agency. After obtaining her doctoral degree, Dr. Wash was hired by the city of Chicago as a mental health director. She worked for the City of Chicago Department of Public Health Division of Mental Health for eighteen years. During this time, she developed EMAGES by working a twelve- to fourteen-hour week. Seven and half hours she worked for the city of Chicago, and four to five hours, including weekends, she worked to develop EMAGES. Dr. Wash also taught part-time at Chicago State University in the psychology department for most of the 1990s.

Dr. Wash retired from the City of Chicago Department of Public Health Division of Mental Health in 2012. As the founder and CEO of EMAGES,

Inc., she is known for her non-traditional and culturally specific treatment approaches and techniques, as well as for her focus on providing an avenue for African American students entering the treatment fields to be trained in techniques and methods that are designed based around the history, culture, and backgrounds of African American clients. Dr. Wash is active in the African American community and is an active member of the Association of Black Psychologists, the Community of African American Mental Health Professionals, and the International Institute of Black Addiction Professionals. In her spare time, Dr. Wash enjoys bowling and traveling. She is the mother of a daughter, Nzinga Akila Knight, and the grandmother of DeShawn Wiley.

CPSIA information can be obtained
at www.ICGtesting.com
Printed in the USA
LVHW091317180521
687772LV00001B/4